ID4
INDEPENDENCE DAY

Rachel Aberly & Volker Engel

THE MAKING OF INDEPENDENCE DAY
ISBN 1 85286 731 0

Published by
Titan Books
42-44 Dolben Street
London SE1 0UP

First edition August 1996
10 9 8 7 6 5 4 3

British Library Cataloguing-in-Publication Data. A catalogue record for
this book is available from the British Library.

Design by Chris Teather.
Production by Bob Kelly.

Independence Day photos by Myles Aronwitz, Claudette Barius, Volker
Engel, Melissa Moseley and Benedikt Niemann. *Universal Soldier* and
StarGate photographs courtesy of the BFI.

DEDICATIONS:

Dean, Roland, Ute, Peter, Bill and the folks at Fox. Thanks for inviting
me along — Rachel.

To Roland Emmerich, who had the courage to let myself and a handful
of highly talented students from Ludwigsburg contribute to this
wonderful project — Volker.

The Publishers would also like to thank Steve Manners, Debbie Olshan
and Jennifer Sebree at Twentieth Century Fox for their tireless help with
this project, and everyone at the *Independence Day* production office.

Printed and bound in Great Britain by Stephens and George Ltd, Merthyr
Industrial Estate, Dowlais, Merthyr Tydfil.

Contents

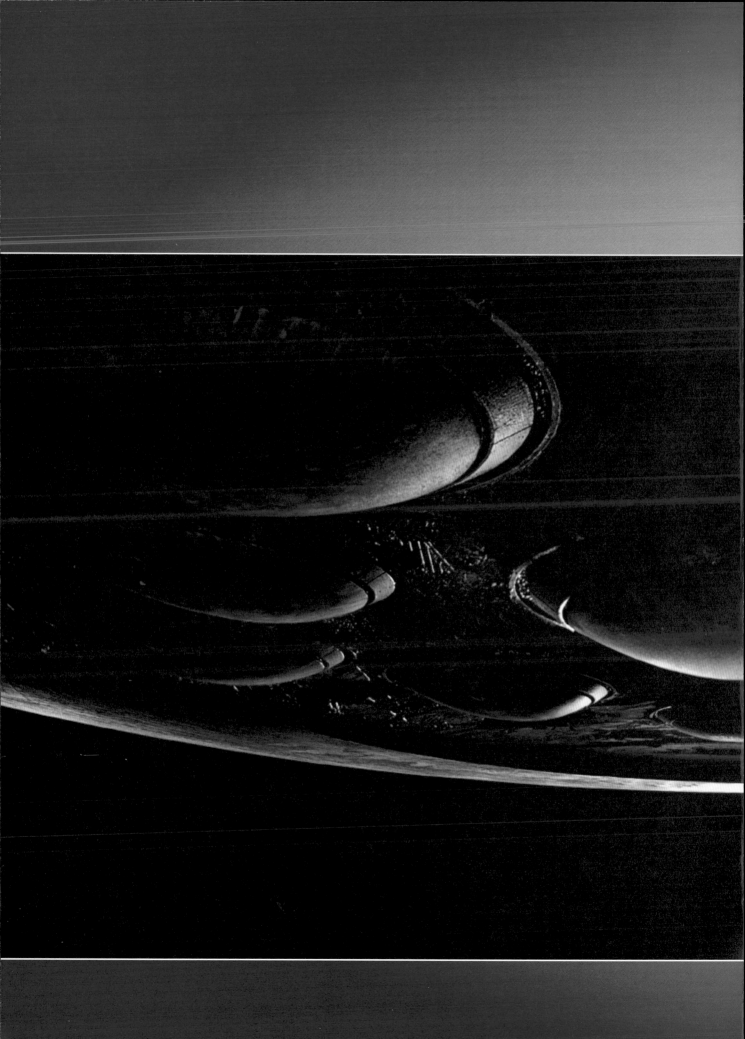

Countdown

An Idea Is Born

What if one morning, you woke up and, like every other morning, glanced up to say a sleepy hello to the nascent sun? What if that familiar yellow orb didn't wink back at you? Instead, the dark underbelly of a mammoth spaceship hovered in the sky, swallowing the sun, turning day to night. What if?

This monumental 'what if' intrigued the film-making team of director Roland Emmerich and producer Dean Devlin, becoming the basis for *Independence Day*. According to Devlin, when they were promoting their previous film, *StarGate*, a reporter asked Emmerich if he believed in aliens. Emmerich replied that he did not, adding, "'I believe in fantasy. I believe in the great 'What if?' What if tomorrow morning you walked out of your door and these enormous spaceships hovered over every single city in the world? What would you do? Wouldn't that be the most exciting day in the history of mankind?' Of course, he then walked over to me and said, 'I think I've got our next movie.'"

As *StarGate* opened, to record numbers at the box office and critical observations that the film marked the return of the science fiction genre, Devlin and Emmerich travelled to Mexico to pen *Independence Day*. They completed the script in thirty days, sent it out for consideration on a

Thursday at noon and by Friday at 10pm Twentieth Century Fox had purchased the screenplay and greenlit the movie. By the following Monday, *Independence Day* was in pre-production.

Just as *StarGate* paid homage to the ancient Egyptian epics of the past, *Independence Day* reflects another bygone genre, the multi-character disaster film.

"Roland and I are fans of the disaster films of the seventies," Devlin says. "When we were writing *Independence Day*, we talked about the kinds of films we don't get to see any more and thought it would be great to revive that genre. The disaster films, of which Irwin Allen was the king, allowed us to see a wide group of characters that represented different aspects of the population. Because there was no single hero, the audience was never quite sure about the ending. The disaster films offered the audience an opportunity to enjoy a fulfilling, fun, popcorn kind of movie. An event film that was not totally predictable."

Emmerich and Devlin knew that to make the disaster film enticing to contemporary audiences, they had to bring a new twist to it. "In *Independence Day*, that becomes the alien invasion," explains Devlin. "The appearance of the spaceships serves as the worldwide, international disaster that unites the planet."

The alien aspect coupled with the disaster genre predetermined that the movie would also feature dazzling special effects. This unique combination allowed Devlin and Emmerich the opportunity to achieve their primary goal as film-makers: to entertain in the most novel way possible.

A Unique Duo

Right: *Producer Dean Devlin.*

Below: *Kurt Russell in StarGate.*

Opposite: *Roland Emmerich and (below) Vivica A. Fox.*

A unique film-making duo, director Roland Emmerich and producer Dean Devlin also co-wrote *Independence Day*. They worked in the same capacities on *StarGate* and, as Devlin points out, it is a relationship well-suited to such event pictures.

"As writers, we can come up with ideas like giant spaceships hovering over much of the planet, but as the director and the producer, we know that we can deliver the kind of amazing effects required to produce that. If we can't, then we re-write. So, it becomes an extremely practical arrangement."

Although Emmerich has established himself as an expert science fiction auteur, he confesses that the genre, *per se*, didn't captivate him until he experienced it cinematically.

"I was never a kid who read a lot of sci-fi novels. It wasn't until I was at film school that I realised that science fiction movies was something that I enjoyed very much. *Star Wars*, *Close Encounters of the Third Kind*, those movies pretty much changed my life. Those are the kind of movies that influenced me to make the kind of films I do... I'm trying to reach a certain audience that I was a part of when I first saw those movies."

The amazing possibilities suggested in those films tantalised Emmerich, causing him to look at science fiction in an entirely different light.

"Those movies made me realise that I was very drawn to 'what if' stories and sci-fi is a perfect way to examine that. I'm always coming up with plots that have fantastic elements, I'm drawn to that. The other thing about science fiction movies is that they

allow you to create entirely new worlds, which requires building sets and models and stuff like that. I always wanted to become a production designer, so that's interesting to me."

Emmerich maintains that the movies provide the perfect means to express science fiction storytelling.

"The simple fact is that we constantly want to tell each other fairy tales and when we're telling each other stories, we usually embellish them. Like, if you had a little car accident on the way to work, you make a bigger deal out of it by the time you get to the office. We try to make it a more exciting story. In films, we have to entertain in an even bigger way than that and science fiction provides scenarios for the biggest possible stories. But, it all comes from fairy tales, the stories we tell each other around the camp fire, trying to entertain each other. We just have to do it in a larger way in films, to justify people going out of the house, getting in the car and driving to a movie theatre."

Roland Emmerich's first American film was the 1992 hit *Universal Soldier*, starring Jean-Claude Van Damme, which Emmerich directed and Devlin co-wrote. He was initially reluctant to helm the project until it was agreed that Devlin could re-work the script.

Emmerich began his career in his native Germany. As a youth, he pursued painting and sculpting, studying production design while at film school in Munich. He segued into directing and his student film, *The Noah's Ark Principle*, went on to open the 1984 Berlin Film Festival. The feature became a huge success and was sold to more than twenty countries.

wrote with Oliver Eberle, and starred Michael Paré, Malcolm McDowell, Lisa Eichhorn and Dean Devlin. Devlin would eventually become a partner in Centropolis, as well as Emmerich's producer and co-writer. *Moon 44*, set in 2018, featured 100 days of special effects and thirty full-sized interiors as it detailed the battle over the last mineral rights in space between rival mining corporations.

Dean Devlin began his career as an actor, featuring in James Kirkwood's Broadway production of *There Must Be a Pony*. He appeared in numerous film and television projects, with notable performances on *LA Law* and the short-lived CBS series *Hard Copy*. While working with Emmerich as an actor in *Moon 44*, the two found they enjoyed similar movies and Devlin's writing ability impressed the director as much as his acting. Devlin subsequently gave up acting to write and produce movies with Emmerich.

Above: *Director Roland Emmerich.*

Right: *Devlin and Emmerich's first full collaboration, Universal Soldier.*

Emmerich subsequently formed his own production company, Centropolis Film Productions, and under its aegis, produced his subsequent movies. His next film was *Making Contact* (aka *Joey*), the tale of a boy suffering from his father's death who finds a way to communicate with him via his toys. The movie showcased Emmerich's vast knowledge of special effects. This was followed by *Ghost Chase*, a comedy he co-wrote with Oliver Eberle about two young film fanatics and their struggle for success in Hollywood. Emmerich also served as producer on *Eye of the Storm*, which starred Dennis Hopper, and directed the futuristic action-adventure movie *Moon 44*, which he co-

The Emmerich/Devlin partnership evolved into a singular artistic association. As Bill Pullman, who plays the President, elaborates: "There is an unusual bond between Dean and Roland. They shared a lot of roles, the boundaries between their responsibilities were not absolutely fixed and that can only happen when there is a certain degree of good chemistry. Their relationship was very subtle and interesting, how they thought, the way they agreed or disagreed. In the very rare times when they would have opposite points of view, they often wouldn't negate each other, which presents a kind of truth that can be rich for an actor to respond to."

Will Smith, playing Captain Steven Hiller, comments that "it helps to have the writer, director and producer on set at all times, especially in a film that is so full of effects. Dean or Roland were always available to answer any questions. Roland, in particular, is so technically well-informed and was always willing to bring us into that world, to share it with us. The great thing about Roland is that he knows exactly what he wants. He was absolutely positive in his vision and that really opened it up for you to toss in a little something to take it to the next level. He provided the springboard for the actors to bring the words to life in their own way."

Jeff Goldblum, cast as David Levinson, the affable, eccentric computer genius, adds that Emmerich and Devlin "are very imaginative and this movie came straight from their hearts. It's very personal for them, I think, and when you're on set, you can feel their passion for it, their involvement, and it's infectious. They fostered an atmosphere that was kind, generous, fun and collaborative."

Above left:
Dean Devlin.

Above right:
Devlin with Jeff Goldblum.

The Production Team

Right: Visual effects supervisor, Volker Engel. In the background (from left to right): VFX production supervisor, Bob Hurrie, VFX director of photography, Anna Foerster, and camera assistant, Marc Brown.

Any film depends heavily on a long list of collaborators, and this is particularly true for a film of *Independence Day*'s scope. The effects team, headed by visual effects supervisors Volker Engel and Doug Smith, the latter specialising in motion control, was kept especially busy.

While studying graphic design, Engel met writer/director Roland Emmerich and suspended his studies to work on Emmerich's independent science fiction feature *Moon 44*. Engel initially created some of the film's models and ultimately served as the visual effects supervisor. He rejoined the film-maker on *Universal Soldier*, returning to school afterwards, to

complete his studies. He subsequently took a job at a film school near Stuttgart and spent two years teaching visual effects, primarily model work and animation. Many of his students would ultimately comprise the effects departments which created the spectacular visual sequences in *Independence Day*.

Doug Smith began his career at the famed Industrial Light and Magic, where he worked on *Star Wars*. He went on to become a partner in Apogee Productions, a breakthrough effects house that spearheaded developments in film emulsions, lighting, matte techniques, effects projection and motion control. The latter would become his domain on *Independence Day*, headquartered in Building 45 at Hughes Aircraft.

The German contingent of the visual effects team began to come together when Engel received a call from Emmerich.

"Around November of 1994, I got a call from Roland," Engel recalls. "He said that he and Dean were preparing a script and it wasn't finished, but he wanted to double-check if I would be willing to supervise the visual effects. I said, 'Yes, definitely,' and two months later Roland called back and asked me to look for some people I wanted to work with. So, I looked around and tried to find the most talented people who would also have the best chemistry for the kind of teamwork that would be required."

Many of the students Engel had either taught or met at film school in Germany came to mind. He knew they were talented, original thinkers, unconstrained by conventional wisdom that dictates the way effects films are 'supposed' to be done.

He also realised that the rigours of school trained them to endure long, often tedious hours: "For instance, I chose Anna Foerster and Philipp Timme to be directors of photography for visual effects because I knew they were incredibly capable and I knew they would be able to handle very complicated, time-consuming, detailed work."

For some of the animation, Engel turned to the German trio, Hartmut Engel, Benedikt Niemann and Stefan Herrman: "They were extremely hard-working and I was really impressed by their talent."

Engel also brought in Conny Fauser-Rumelin, whom he had met while studying graphic design. Hauser ended up contributing to some key visual sequences involving the reveal of the spaceship through what became known as the Phenomenon.

Two additional Germans to join the crew, Marc Weigert and Nikolaus Kraemer were already based in Los Angeles. They had worked with Engel previously, on a television movie that the Academy produced for a German station.

"It was an extremely complex project, with seventeen effects shots, including space stations, Earth matte paintings and a lot of model work," Engel says. "I chose Marc and Nikolaus to produce these effects and we came in under budget, on time, with three times more material than was anticipated. Soon after this, Marc and Nik decided to build their own company in Los Angeles. I hired them for *Independence Day* and they did the complicated breakdowns and listings for the effects shots."

Opposite below:
Visual effects supervisor, Doug Smith.

Below left:
Visual effects director of photography, Philipp Timme, who shot the city destruction.

Below right:
Visual effects director of photography, Anna Foerster, who shot all the Destroyers.

It Came from Outer Space

Hollywood has always been fascinated by the possibility of alien beings visiting our planet. Here are just a few of the best, and worst, examples of alien invasion movies:

The Thing from Another World (1951). Directed by Christian Nyby and produced by Howard Hawks. James Arness makes a notable appearance as The Thing in one of the first movies to revolve around an unfriendly alien.

The Day the Earth Stood Still (1951). Directed by Robert Wise and starring Michael Rennie and Patricia Neal. Alien Klaatu comes to Earth to warn man that he must put an end to all warfare. If his message is ignored, Earth will be destroyed.

The War of the Worlds (1953). Directed by Byron Haskin and starring Gene Barry, based on the novel by H. G. Wells. A flying saucer lands near a small American town, carrying hostile Martians out to destroy the world. The still impressive special effects won an Academy Award.

It Came from Outer Space (1953). Directed in 3-D by Jack Arnold and starring Richard Carlson. This time aliens crash-land in the Arizona desert, near another small American town, and have the ability to transform into human form.

Invasion of the Body Snatchers (1956). Directed by Don Siegel and starring Kevin McCarthy. Yet another small American town is invaded by creatures from outer space, only this time they arrive in strange pods.

The Man Who Fell to Earth (1976). Directed by Nicolas Roeg and starring David Bowie. Glam rock star Bowie makes a very credible extraterrestrial, who comes to Earth in search of water for his parched planet.

Close Encounters of the Third Kind (1977). Directed by Steven Spielberg and starring Richard Dreyfuss and Melinda Dillon, with a cameo by Dr J. Allen Hynek, the late head of the Centre for UFO Studies. Dreyfuss plays the quintessential Everyman who is mysteriously solicited to become one of the first humans to meet aliens.

E.T. (1982). Again directed by Steven Spielberg, and featuring probably the most famous visitor from outer space, alongside the human cast of Henry Thomas, Drew Barrymore and Dee Wallace Stone. The film Spielberg calls 'closest to my own heart' tells of a boy who befriends an adorable alien, lost in the wilds of suburbia.

And not forgetting...

Plan 9 from Outer Space (1959). Often cited as the Worst Film Ever Made, Ed Wood's inept SF adventure is actually a lot of fun. A band of unique aliens try to conquer the Earth by resuscitating the dead. Features Bela Lugosi's final appearance, for all of ten seconds. He died during filming and his part was taken over by a body double who stood a good foot taller. ■

FROM OUT OF SPACE .... A WARNING AND AN ULTIMATUM!

THE DAY THE EARTH STOOD STILL

MICHAEL RENNIE · PATRICIA NEAL · HUGH MARLOWE

Working closely with the effects department, and very much playing a key role in *Independence Day*'s success, was the model-making team. Mike Joyce, who headed the model department, has worked on a number of big movies, including *Batman Forever*, but none, he admits, were as overwhelming as *Independence Day*.

Over the course of production, Joyce's staff would include twenty-five model-makers, three sculptors, numerous production assistants and four painters.

Most of Joyce's miniatures eventually ended up with Joe Viskocil and his pyro-effects team, who worked with visual effects supervisor Volker Engel. The vast majority of these models would be blasted to bits in various destruction shots by the team at Building 35 at Hughes Aircraft.

With all these effects, the CGI department, headed by digital effects producer Tricia Ashford, was obviously going to be kept pretty busy. So busy, in fact, that Tricia and computer graphics supervisor Tara Turner needed to assemble a core team of co-

digital effects producer Steven Puri, digital production manager Craig Mumma and CG supervisor Joe Francis. Their work eventually multiplied to the extent that they had to utilise the services of a number of effects houses.

The production designer role was also going to prove essential to the film's success, especially when it came to creating a believable alien world. This task fell to Oliver Scholl and Patrick Tatopoulos, who were greatly aided in shaping the film's look by leading cinematographer Karl Walter Lindenlaub.

Other key behind-the-scenes personnel whose contributions would undoubtedly enhance the final product include mechanical effects supervisor Clay Pinney, stunt co-ordinator Dan Bradley and his team, and costume designer Joseph Porro. Together, they all played a vital role in the production of *Independence Day*

Left: *Pyro supervisor, Joe Viskocil, prepares an F-18 model for an explosion in the first dogfight.*

Below: *Model shop supervisor, Mike Joyce, and model-maker, Ken Swenson, examine the lunar lander used in the movie's opening sequence.*

Who's Who

Right: Roland Emmerich.

In keeping with multi-character disaster films, *Independence Day* features a broad, ensemble cast. Each character plays a vital, unique part in the battle to outwit and defeat the alien force.

"We tried to find the perfect actor for each part, to assemble a cast that was balanced, because we wanted the audience to have the feeling that each character was equally important," Emmerich explains. "So, in the face of disaster, it was possible that any of them could die and that losing any one of them would be a big loss. That obviously depended a lot on the actors we cast."

"The tradition of the disaster film, and even the World War Two movies like *The Longest Day*, was to have strong actors," Devlin adds. "Because the better the actor is, the more the audiences get involved with the character and then they care about the adventure they go on. We really wanted to go for the best actors available and, fortunately, we have an exceptional cast."

Although *Independence Day* is an ensemble picture, Devlin regards the characters played by Will Smith (Captain Steven Hiller, a crackerjack Marine pilot), Bill Pullman (the young, earnest President who quite literally defends his country) and Jeff Goldblum (David Levinson, the affable computer/math genius who figures out the aliens' deadly game) as the film's heart, soul and brains.

"Each of these actors used their unique strengths to emphasise these three aspects, which I don't think were in the script originally. I think they originated in the performances. Will Smith was clearly the heart of the movie, the Everyman in America, the good GI Joe, like you would have seen in the old World War Two movies. Bill Pullman's President, as the soul, was a man of honour who has to make some very tough decisions in dire circumstances and becomes a hero in the process. Jeff Goldblum, the brains, is so terrific at playing brilliant, quirky, endearing characters and I think he outdid himself in this."

In fact, Devlin confesses that working with the entire group of actors proved to be "the most exciting thing, by far for me, during the course of the production. A writer has an experience when he is alone at the computer. The interpretations and colours these immensely gifted actors brought to that experience, creating moments and transcending character and situation, was fun to watch and to nurture."

David Levinson
Computer wizard
Julius Levinson
David's father
Constance Spano
David's ex-wife
Communications Director
Marty Gilbert
David's work colleague

Thomas J. Whitmore
President of the
United States
Marilyn Whitmore
The First Lady
Patricia Whitmore
The President's daughter

Capt Steven Hiller
Marine pilot
Jasmine Dubrow
Steve's girlfriend
Dylan Dubrow
Jasmine's son
Capt Jimmy Wilder
Steve's friend
Fellow pilot

General Grey
Chairman of the Joint
Chiefs of Staff
Secretary Nimziki
Secretary of Defense
Dr Brakish Okun
Head Area 51 scientist

Russell Casse
Crop-duster pilot
Miguel Casse
Troy Casse
Alicia Casse
Russell's children

Jeff GOLDBLUM
DAVID LEVINSON

Jeff Goldblum plays the quirky, altruistic computer genius David Levinson, whose passion for chess and for his ex-wife lead him on a journey towards the alien force.

"Jeff Goldblum is our eccentric cable repairman, though that's actually a joke," says Devlin. "He is a satellite technician, but his father constantly refers to him as a cable repairman because he works for the local cable company in New York City. Because he works with satellite transmissions, he's actually the first to discover a code the aliens have embedded into our system and the first to realise what is about to happen."

Emmerich adds: "When we were writing the script, we constantly said, 'So, who can do this?' All of a sudden, we realised Jeff Goldblum was totally the one. I have seen no other actor who can explain technical things as convincingly as Jeff can. He makes the information a part of the character. There's also a kind of quirkiness to him, which gives the character so much more than what's on the page."

Goldblum describes David as "a humble and loveable cable man. He is a smart guy who is idealistic, passionate and suspicious of big institutions like the government. He is also very romantic and loves his ex-wife, even though she has gone to work for the President. That love gives him strength and propels him to try to save her. This brings him to the White House, which sets everything in motion."

No stranger to science fiction, having played both a scientist whose experiments turn him into a giant fly and an expert in chaos theory who applies it to new-age dinosaurs, Goldblum was drawn to *Independence Day* by its underlying humanitarian themes.

"I like what the movie stands for. It's about how different people can join together for a common, grand, noble purpose and the best about them comes out in the process. The alien threat brings out our sense of brotherhood and responsibility, it causes us to connect with what's really important."

Goldblum shares his character's conscientiousness and amiable attitude. His relentless cheer manifested itself in song and he regularly crooned in-between takes. This musical habit frequently brought a rueful smile to Emmerich's face, as he

shook his head incredulously. Despite his vast knowledge of the strange and wondrous world of special effects, Emmerich had never seen anything like this. Harvey Fierstein, who played Goldblum's boss, notes that "his energy was just unbelievable. I was laying on the floor one night, at about 11:30. I couldn't even lift my arms again to do anything else and he was dancing around the room, singing forties love songs. He was amazing."

Goldblum moved to New York at the age of seventeen to study acting at the Neighbourhood Playhouse with Sanford Meisner, and in less than a year Joseph Papp cast him in the New York Shakespeare Festival production of *The Two Gentlemen of Verona*. He made his film début in Michael Winner's *Death Wish* and was then cast by Robert Altman as a twenty-year-old executive in *California Split*. Altman then cast him as the mysterious biker/ magician in *Nashville*.

Goldblum's subsequent screen appearances include Paul Mazursky's *Next Stop, Greenwich Village*, Woody Allen's *Annie Hall*, Joan Micklin Silver's *Between the Lines* and Alan Rudolph's *Remember My Name*. Philip Kaufman's *Invasion of the Body Snatchers* and *The Right Stuff* then led to starring roles in *The Big Chill, Threshold, The Adventures of Buckaroo Banzai, Earth Girls Are Easy, Silverado, Into the Night, The Fly, The Tall Guy, Twisted Obsession, Fathers and Sons* and *Deep Cover*.

More recently, Goldblum has appeared in the boxing satire, *The Great White Hype*, acted with Hugh Grant in Chris Columbus' comedy *Nine Months* and starred as an acerbic, witty scientist in Steven Spielberg's smash-hit dinosaur adventure *Jurassic Park*, which has become the highest grossing motion picture of all time.

Judd HIRSCH
JULIUS LEVINSON

David Levinson's father, the irascible, outspoken Julius Levinson, is portrayed by Judd Hirsch. An engaging personality on set, Hirsch regaled the cast and crew with anecdotes and jokes, drawing on his varied experiences on the New York stage and in many memorable movies. He and Jeff Goldblum, both fond of improvisation, regularly sent Emmerich and Devlin in to fits of laughter at the video playback monitor.

Devlin notes that "Julius is a curmudgeonly, wickedly funny New Yorker, and although Judd isn't curmudgeonly, he is definitely hilarious. He is one of my favourite actors on the planet. Some people initially thought he was too young to play Jeff's father, but I remembered him playing an eighty-year-old man on Broadway, in *I'm Not Rappaport*. His genius is that he has the ability to be very funny in one moment and incredibly touching in the next, which was very important for the character. Roland and I met with him in New York and after five minutes, Roland turned to me and said, 'That's Julius.'"

Emmerich, in fact, was one of those people who had had reservations about Hirsch as Goldblum's dad, simply because the actor "looks really good for someone who is sixty."

"We were looking for somebody who could believably play Jeff's dad, and that was not easy,"

Emmerich says. "When we met Judd in New York, he told us, 'I'm totally the right age to play him, because I'm sixty.' I said, 'But you don't look like you're sixty, so we'll have to make you look it.' And that's what we did, with make-up. We really had to make him quite older looking."

Hirsch describes Julius as "candid, blunt, honest… he habitually says whatever is on his mind. He loves his son, David, but thinks he's wasting his intelligence and potential working at this cable repair job and tells him so. Yet he sticks by David, believes in him and defends him, and that is also due to his love for his son. It also has something to do with his underlying distrust of the stuff the government is telling them. Actually, he's a very sensible character."

Hirsch was born in New York, studied engineering at The City College of New York and architecture at Cooper Union before turning to acting. He then began to study at the American Academy of

Dramatic Arts and at the HB Studio in Manhattan.

An accomplished stage and screen actor, Hirsch is probably best known for his role on the long running classic television series, *Taxi*. His portrayal of cabby Alex Reiger earned him two Best Actor Emmy awards and a nomination every season of the show's run. From 1988 to 1992, he starred in the American version of the quirky ensemble comedy series, *Dear John*, for which he won the Golden Globe for Best Actor.

Hirsch's film credits include *King of the Gypsies*, *Ordinary People* (for which he garnered an Academy Award nomination), *Without a Trace*, *Teachers*, *The Goodbye People* and *Running on Empty*.

Harvey FIERSTEIN
MARTY GILBERT

The incorrigible Harvey Fierstein plays Marty Gilbert, David Levinson's harried boss at Compact Cable. Often frustrated by David's quirky outlook, Marty genuinely likes him. Moreover, he is completely aware of his employee's brilliance and realises that he is truly lucky to have such a genius labouring at a modest cable company. Devlin notes that "while he is an incredible businessman, he doesn't know too much about the technical end and relies heavily on David." Fierstein routinely supplied his own unique brand of comic relief throughout the production, especially during the scene in which Marty has a close, brief and untimely encounter with the aliens. He practised several different responses, including the one he modelled after a horrified fifties diva, all of which amused the cast and crew.

The list of actors attached to *Independence Day*, along with the chance to work with Emmerich, initially attracted Fierstein to the film: "I said, 'Oh, to be in a movie with all these people would be just incredible' and it was. All my scenes were with Jeff Goldblum, who was a doll, but I got to meet some of the other people and their company was just divine. I'd never met Roland before, but I'd heard from a couple people that he was fun to work with and that I'd have a really good time and I did, definitely."

One of Fierstein's greatest challenges during the course of the film began with his feet: "I had to run a lot. I had to chase Jeff Goldblum on a bicycle and the shoes they gave me were too tight. After an hour of chasing him on the bike, I finally said, 'If you would like me to live through this shoot, you'll let me wear my own sneakers', and so they did."

Fierstein made his mark on Broadway as both writer and actor in the acclaimed *Torch Song Trilogy*, which he also toured to Los Angeles and London. He also appeared in the film version of the play. Other notable movie credits include Woody Allen's *Bullets Over Broadway*, *Dr Jekyll and Ms Hyde*, *White Lies*, a scene-stealing role in *Mrs Doubtfire*, *The Harvest* and *Garbo Talks*, among others.

Among his television credits are the HBO movie *Tidy Endings*, the CBS series *Daddy's Girls*, on which he was a series regular, guest-starring roles on *Murder, She Wrote*, *The Simpsons*, *Cheers* and *Miami Vice*, and the ABC specials *In the Shadow of Love* and *TV or Not TV*. Other stage credits take in the Broadway production of *Safe Sex* and the off-Broadway production of *The Haunted Host*.

Margaret COLIN
CONSTANCE SPANO

The character of Constance Spano, the President's feisty Communications Director and the ex-wife of David Levinson, was a key part; she served as the link between the answer to the alien problem and its eventual solution. It also called for an actress who could credibly convey an ambitious, no-nonsense woman who was also ingratiating and admirable. The casting search for this actress stretched well into filming, and two days prior to her first scenes Devlin and Emmerich still had not found the perfect person.

Dean Devlin says, "Margaret Colin plays the Director of Communications at the White House. She has been the President's right-hand person since he started his campaign. She is also the ex-wife of Jeff Goldblum's character. While they are still in love with each other, their careers have taken them in opposite directions. The events of the movie bring them back together.

"We looked at several actresses for the part, but nobody really had all the aspects we wanted. Roland refused to compromise and had absolute faith we'd find her. In fact, we cast Margaret two days before her first scenes in front of the cameras. We asked her to come to read for the part in Wendover and told her to pack a bag for at least a two week stay, just in case."

"Margaret was the only one who convinced us that she could play that tough aspect, someone who could quit her marriage for a job at the White House, but still be a sympathetic character," Emmerich adds.

Colin defends Constance, explaining that her career just slowly began to dominate her life, causing her to ignore or repress other characteristics.

"Constance is a good woman... smart, opinionated, ambitious. The alien crisis forces her to examine other aspects of her personality, the nurturing, caring side. She is just not as familiar with it. She loves her ex-husband David, but she loves her career too. She had to make a choice, like many women, between a great job and a marriage she considered to have no future. I believe that David also changes because of the alien situation, becomes more assertive and she realises how much she cares for him."

After *Independence Day*, Colin began production on *The Devil's Own*, alongside Harrison Ford and Brad Pitt. Her additional film credits include *Amos and Andrew*, as the quintessential wealthy bigot, *True Believer*, playing a private eye, opposite James Woods and Robert Downey Jr, *Something Wild*, directed by Jonathan Demme, as Ray Liotta's

unique, spiky-haired girlfriend, as well as roles in *Terminal Velocity*, *The Butcher's Wife*, *Like Father, Like Son*, *Three Men and a Baby*, and her first feature, *Pretty in Pink*.

On television, she enjoyed a recurring role on the series *Chicago Hope*, as the dedicated doctor who discovers that she has a terminal illness. Her stint on *Chicago Hope* reunited her with actor Hector Elizondo, with whom she starred in the acclaimed series, *Foley Square*, produced by Diane English. Her additional television credits include *The Wright Verdicts*, *Double Rush*, *Goodnight, Sweet Wife: Murder in Boston*, *Traveling Man* and *The Return of Sherlock Holmes*. Colin also starred as a series regular on *Sibs* and *Leg Work*.

BILL PULLMAN
PRESIDENT WHITMORE

The pivotal role of President Whitmore went to Bill Pullman. An important part, the President had to embody several characteristics. He is a commander in chief, struggling in Washington, frustrated by murky politics that stymie a one-time military official who is more accustomed to clear

objectives and agendas. Pullman also had to portray a family man, whose life is thrown into turmoil by the alien arrival.

Devlin asserts that "Bill Pullman is one of the great surprises of the film. I think people will see him in a whole new light. He is funny, charismatic, strong; a real, old-fashioned leading man. As President of the United States, he is complicated, a former fighter pilot, a hero of the Gulf War who used that celebrity to propel him into politics. But, he's an outsider, doesn't play the Washington games well. So, at the beginning of the movie, his place in the polls is dropping rapidly. He's a good, decent American, though, and the alien crisis becomes the thing that allows him to prove it."

"We had a long discussion about the President," recalls Emmerich. "We wrote the part for a President who was too young for the job, that was the character description. And then we went looking for him. And then we found Bill and went even younger than we'd originally thought, because we felt he'd play the part very well. Bill can be very, very funny, he has a great sense of humour about himself. He also has this other side, which is really much more the hero figure. We thought both these things were good for the President. In fact, we called him Mr President on the set."

The opportunity to play this President intrigued Pullman. "There's that point when every first-grade teacher says to the class, 'Any one of you could become President of the United States.' This was my opportunity," he jokes. "Seriously, I wanted to do the film because it reminded me of a Saturday afternoon movie, a real entertaining audience event. I

liked the character because this President is human. He is complicated, fallible, but unapologetically a hero. He reminds me of the kind of roles William Holden played in those World War Two movies."

Pullman's President isn't modelled after any one head of state in particular. However, he claims that "I did listen to some of the great speeches on CD, I read some books like *The Commanders* by Bob Woodward and I watched that documentary on the Clinton campaign, *The War Room*. But, for the rest of it, President Whitmore's character is shaped by the nature of what is required of him."

Pullman describes Whitmore as "a man who is a humanist and yet able to make some tough decisions in the face of incredible crisis and loss, a loss that is both national and personal." The role gave Pullman a deeper respect for the office, but, he adds, "I am very thankful that this was just a fictional part to play, because I think you'd have to be a little bit of a

junkie for abuse to be the actual President."

Bill Pullman starred in two of the most popular films to open in the summer of 1995, appearing with Sandra Bullock in the romantic comedy *While You Were Sleeping* and opposite several computer-generated ghosts in Amblin Entertainment's *Casper*. He also appeared with Meg Ryan as her ill-fated fiancé in the hit film *Sleepless in Seattle*, acted opposite Jodie Foster in *Sommersby* and played an avenging husband in *Malice*, alongside Nicole Kidman and Alec Baldwin. Further starring roles include the ultimate bad-seed boyfriend with Ellen DeGeneres in *Mr Wrong* and a troubled jazz musician in David Lynch's upcoming *Lost Highway*.

Pullman made his screen début in 1986 in *Ruthless People*, after working for several years in New York, studying acting and performing off-Broadway and with regional theatres. Following *Ruthless People*, Pullman starred in *Spaceballs*, *The Serpent and the Rainbow*, *The Accidental Tourist* and *Sibling Rivalry*. Other credits include *Wyatt Earp*, *The Favor*, *Singles* and *Crazy in Love*.

Mary McDONNELL
MARILYN WHITMORE

The First Lady, Marilyn Whitmore, was inspired by the actress who plays her, Mary McDonnell. "When we were writing the script, we thought, who would you imagine as the First Lady? Mary McDonnell was who we came up with," recalls Emmerich. "Then it was really weird, because we had to call her up and say, 'So, Mary, would you want to be the First Lady?' She said yes, she was immediately sure. It was great, because we had this vision where we thought it would be perfect if she did it, but we weren't certain she would."

Dean Devlin adds: "Mary McDonnell plays the First Lady and she is fiercely independent. She and the President love each other dearly and part of their story-line is their struggle to find each other through this disaster. Mary was a gift for us. She really had such great enthusiasm and a great love for the part."

McDonnell was very flattered by the film-makers' interest and quite taken by the First Lady they

created: "She's a very responsible, active First Lady. She and the President have a very good marriage. She's the mother of one and she's a woman who enjoys life. She feels passionate about a number of issues, but I think she has fun with it. She is not a woman who is particularly happy to stay at home. So, she doesn't.

"I think that part of what she represents in the film is the idea of family and separation, that vulnerability we carry with us on a daily basis. That at any time, anything could happen and you could be separated from your loved ones. But she is also the First Lady, so she has to stay cool. Still, she is a mother trying to get home. That's really her story."

McDonnell is a two-time Oscar nominee. She received a Best Actress nomination for her performance in John Sayles's acclaimed *Passion Fish*, as a wheelchair-bound, acid-tongued soap opera actress, and a Best Supporting Actress nomination for her

stunning turn as the white woman raised by the Sioux tribe in Kevin Costner's *Dances With Wolves*. She also received the 1991 Movie Award and a Golden Globe nomination for her work in *Dances With Wolves*. Other feature credits include *Sneakers*, Lawrence Kasdan's urban drama *Grand Canyon*, *Blue Chips*, *Tiger Warsaw* and John Sayles's *Matewan*. McDonnell also starred in *Mariette in Ecstasy*, for Savoy Pictures.

On television, McDonnell featured opposite Randy Quaid and Sam Elliott in the Showtime movie *Woman Undone* and, in the TNT adaptation of Arthur Miller's *The American Clock*, alongside David Strathairn and John Rubenstein. She also appeared on the TV series *High Society*.

McDonnell's stage work includes leading parts on Broadway playing the title role in Wendy Wasserstein's Pulitzer Prize-winning play, *The Heidi Chronicles*. Her stage performance as the lead in

Darrah Cloud's adaptation of Willa Cather's *Oh, Pioneers* was filmed for American Playhouse and aired on PBS in 1991. She made her New York theatre début in Sam Shepard's Pulitzer Prize-winning *Buried Child* and, in 1981, received an Obie for her performance in Emily Mann's *Still Life*. Other stage credits take in John Patrick Shanley's *Savage in Limbo*, *All Night Long*, *Black Angel*, *A Weekend Near Madison*, *Death of a Miner* and *National Anthem*.

Mae WHITMAN
PATRICIA WHITMORE

Mae Whitman, who portrays the President's daughter Patricia, had already impressed Devlin and Emmerich with her performance in *When a Man Loves a Woman*. However, it was Whitman's reading for the part that really awed Devlin.

"When we cast Mae, it gave me chills. We had been reading a lot of kids for the movie and every time you read children, it's always adorable. After every one leaves, you say, 'Oh, isn't that sweet.' When Mae came in, she read a very emotional scene when Patricia asks about the death of another character and the line was, 'Is she sleeping now?' Mae did the line and it was very touching, but afterwards she said, 'Now, when I say that, do I know she's dead or do I think she's really sleeping?' I thought, how does a seven-year-old come up with a question like that? So I said, 'Well she's really dead and, yeah, you know, but you just don't want to say it.' Mae says, 'Oh, well I would have done it differently. Can I do it again?' She analysed the part with such intelligence and maturity that I knew we just had to have her."

In addition to *When a Man Loves a Woman*, Whitman has appeared in *Bye, Bye Love*, with Paul Reiser, Matthew Modine and Randy Quaid. Her television parts include the young Ashley Judd in the highly-rated NBC mini-series *The Judds*, as well as a co-starring role in *Degree of Guilt*. She has also been in numerous commercials.

WILL SMITH
CAPTAIN STEVEN HILLER

Will Smith plays the role of Captain Steven Hiller, the assured, gifted Marine fighter pilot. The part marked Smith's first character in uniform and his fledgling foray into science fiction. Emmerich notes that he and Devlin always envisioned an African-American in this all-American

hero role and specifically wanted Smith, a choice that became especially appealing to the studio after the outrageous success of the action-adventure *Bad Boys*. However, it was another film that brought the actor to Emmerich and Devlin's attention.

"We saw *Six Degrees of Separation* and thought Will did a hell of a job there. He has this all-American quality about him. He's a guy's guy, but he's so charming and sure of himself that women like him," Emmerich recalls.

Devlin adds: "Captain Hiller is the classic fighter pilot-ace type. He's dreamed his whole life of space exploration, but has not yet been accepted to NASA. In a sense, he's really the heart of the film. Will brought humour and fun to the character, but he also has this innate ability to play the hero. Off-camera as well. During those really hot, long days in the Wendover Salt Flats, his energy and enthusiasm never failed. In fact, one day the sun just got to little Ross Bagley, who was only six and played Dylan. Will sat with him and talked to him, and pretty soon Ross felt better and wanted to go back out and shoot."

The part appealed to Smith for several reasons: "The role was interesting, because it is definitely serious but the character is also funny. Before *Independence Day*, I usually played one or the other. I also was a big fan of the disaster films. I grew up watching them and it was fun to be in one. Captain Hiller is a regular guy, the kind of character I like to play, who finds himself in a very irregular situation. But he's definitely up to it. These aliens, coming to take over the world, run into the United States Marine Corps, specifically Captain Steven Hiller... we basically save the world. He's huge. This

movie is huge. It was a challenge sometimes to act off of special effects that weren't there, but Roland and Dean were great about showing us footage of explosions, which helped. Still, you sort of have to 'extra-act.' You know, if there's supposed to be an explosion that shakes you, but you're pretty much just sitting in your chair and you have to respond to it."

Smith, of course, did encounter one of his alien foes in Wendover, which he envisioned as "about 8'4" and 460 pounds. A really ugly, smelly monster."

Smith starred with Martin Lawrence in the hit action-comedy *Bad Boys*, playing Mike Lowrey, the smooth talking, fashionably dressed half of a duo of unconventional cops. After completing *Independence Day*, he began production on Amblin Entertainment's *Men in Black*, directed by Barry Sonnenfeld and co-starring Tommy Lee Jones.

Smith's motion picture work is highlighted by his critically acclaimed performance in the Oscar-nominated *Six Degrees of Separation*. His film credits also include *Made in America*, starring Whoopi Goldberg and Ted Danson, and *Where the Day Takes You*.

In 1986, Smith and Jeff Townes formed the group, D.J. Jazzy Jeff and The Fresh Prince. They earned the 1988 Grammy Award for Best Rap Performance for 'Parents Just Don't Understand', the hit single from their second album, *He's the DJ, I'm the Rapper*. They also won a Grammy for the single 'Summertime', from their fourth album, *Homebase*, which was released in 1991 and went platinum. In 1992, Smith and Townes were honoured at the NAACP Image Awards as Outstanding Rap Artists.

Smith's musical talent and showmanship led to the creation of the hit NBC series, *The Fresh Prince of Bel-Air*, which has just completed its final season. The NAACP honoured Smith with a subsequent Image Award for his work on this series.

Vivica A. FOX
JASMINE DUBROW

V ivica A. Fox appears as Jasmine Dubrow, a strong-willed single mother, Captain Hiller's girlfriend and a sometime exotic dancer: "I really wanted to play her because she is such a great character, especially for an African-American woman. She is so many things... a single mom, a heroine. She refuses to accept limitations. She's strong, sensitive, tough and really rises to the occasion when she has to."

Independence Day is Fox's first feature film leading role and she was admittedly nervous. However, she had worked with Will Smith previously, on his television show, *The Fresh Prince of Bel-Air*, and that, she says, "made for a certain comfort level, since I already knew him, which was very helpful." The true 'unknown' for Fox was Jasmine's work as an exotic dancer.

"I am definitely not a dancer, so for a month and a half before shooting, I worked out with a choreographer and a trainer every morning. That really helped. We shot the scenes of Jasmine dancing at a real strip joint, at 8.30 in the morning. There I was, standing in front of the crew in a G-string. The train-

ing really helped me to let go and forget myself, to just become Jasmine."

Fox has appeared in such features as *Don't Be a Menace to Society*, *Lowdown Dirty Shame* and *Born on the Fourth of July*. On television, she had a recurring role on the daytime drama *Young and the Restless* and has been a series regular on *Living Dolls*, *Generations*, *In the House* and *Out All Night*. Other television credits include guest starring roles on *The Watcher*, *Family Matters*, *Matlock*, *Beverly Hills 90210*, *Hotel Dicks*, *China Beach* and *Days of Our Lives*. Her stage work includes *In the Abyss of Coney Island* and *Generations of the Dead*, at Los Angeles's Taper Too.

ROSS BAGLEY
DYLAN DUBROW

Ross Bagley, who plays Jasmine's young son Dylan, had already worked on a regular basis with Will Smith, as his cousin on *The Fresh Prince of Bel-Air*, before *Independence Day*. Bagley made his motion picture début in Penelope Spheeris's movie version of *The Little Rascals*, as Buckwheat, and appeared in *An Eye for an Eye* with Sally Field. He also attracted national attention in television commercials for Kix Berry Berry cereal and Oscar Mayer Lunchables. His other television credits include co-hosting the nationally syndicated *United Against Hunger* with Ed Asner and the ABC pilot *Cherry Street South of Main*.

Harry CONNICK JR
CAPTAIN JIMMY WILDER

Harry Connick Jr portrays Captain Jimmy Wilder, a constant jokester and Captain Steven Hiller's best friend. Connick managed to fit *Independence Day* into an extremely busy schedule, which also included a concert tour. With common professional/personal interests in music and a shared appreciation of the absurd, Connick and Smith's off-screen camaraderie reflected their on-screen friend-ship. "Harry's character is really a throwback to the World War Two movies," Devlin says. "He is Captain Hiller's best friend and they are the two best pilots in the squadron. He is a character who simply cannot deal with tension. So, in any kind of pressure situation, he has to crack a joke. Sometimes Captain Hiller appreciates his humour and sometimes it just annoys him, but they are true buddies."

"Will was terrific to work with, a lot of fun, but really professional," Connick recalls. "This was my fourth film and I really enjoyed it, it was a nice change from music. When I read the script, I was really excited about it. It's one of those movies that leave you with a real gung-ho feeling at the end and it was great to be a part of it."

Connick is a three-time Grammy-winning musician, known for his unique New Orleans sound and his contemporary interpretations of jazz and swing standards. He has also successfully parlayed his talent into several memorable film roles. His first brush with the film world was Rob Reiner's romantic comedy *When Harry Met Sally*, which featured several classic, American jazz tunes interpreted by Connick. In 1990, Connick made his acting début in the ensemble feature about the legendary World War Two plane, *Memphis Belle*, directed by Michael Caton-Jones. He went on to appear in *Little Man Tate*, directed by Jodie Foster, who also starred in the film, and portrayed a serial killer in the thriller *Copycat*, opposite Holly Hunter and Sigourney Weaver. In addition to acting in movies, his music has also contributed to them. His song 'I Could Only Whisper Your Name' was included on the soundtrack of the hit film *The Mask*.

PAGE 42 THE MAKING OF INDEPENDENCE DAY

Robert LOGGIA
GENERAL GREY

Actor Robert Loggia was selected to play staid, dignified General Grey, Chairman of the Joint Chiefs of Staff. He has a prior relationship with the President," says Devlin. "He was the President's commander during the Gulf War. They go back a long way and share a unique bond that separates them from the rest of the White House. Loggia adds

a real element of class to the picture. His performance is outstanding. His character is a long-time military man, so he is stoic, controlled, but Loggia also gave him a great deal of warmth."

His presence was vital, Emmerich adds, because the military plays such an important part in the race to defeat the aliens: "General Grey is the link to the military in the movie, so he plays a crucial part. The audience has to believe that he is a real, distinguished military leader and Robert Loggia was really able to do that."

If Loggia's General Grey seems authentic, it's because the actor was inspired by the legendary generals of World War Two: "Well, I was never much of a sci-fi fan when I was growing up. I couldn't really suspend disbelief for the *Buck Rogers* films, the technology just wasn't there yet. I was fifteen when World War Two ended and my heroes were the generals who won the war... Eisenhower, Bradley, Clark and Patton. They were no-nonsense good-guys and there is a lot of that in General Grey. So I tried to model him a bit after these generals, especially Patton."

Loggia, who initially intended to become a journalist, has appeared in many movies, including *Bad Girls*, *Necessary Roughness*, *The Marrying Man*, *Big*, *Prizzi's Honor*, *That's Life*, *Jagged Edge*, *Scarface* and *An Officer and a Gentleman*, among many others. He recently completed David Lynch's *Lost Highway* with his *Independence Day* co-star Bill Pullman. Among his television credits are the Showtime movie *The Right to Remain Silent*, the HBO films *White Mile* and *Afterburn*, and the intriguing Oliver Stone/ABC series *Wild Palms*.

James REBHORN
ALBERT NIMZIKI

James Rebhorn appears as General Grey's nefarious, trigger-happy counterpart, Secretary of Defense Albert Nimziki. Nimziki is as impulsive as General Grey is reserved and, as ex-director of the Central Intelligence Agency, his past is as shady as Grey's is crystal clear. He knows where all the bodies are buried. Not a bad person to have as an ally. Unfortunately, his allegiance, as the movie unfolds, becomes highly questionable.

Rebhorn explains that "Nimziki is very devoted to his office, absolutely to his President and truly believes that the course of action he suggests is the right and proper one to save the country." Although he does not consider Nimziki a 'bad guy', Rebhorn allows that "Nimziki loves power and he loves his authority to wield it, but in his own mind he is a very loyal American. There might be a little Oliver North to him. He is dedicated to his duty, as he defines it. He firmly believes that everything he does is ultimately for the good of the country."

Rebhorn has portrayed a broad range of characters in his career, recently appearing in *Up Close & Personal* opposite Robert Redford and Michelle Pfeiffer, playing Pfeiffer's likeable boss. Other notable film credits include *How to Make an American Quilt*, *Carlito's Way*, *Scent of a Woman*, *Lorenzo's Oil*, *Guarding Tess*, *Regarding Henry*, *White Sands*, *My Cousin Vinny*, *Basic Instinct*, *Shadows & Fog* and *Silkwood*, among many others. On television he has appeared in the acclaimed movie *Sarah Plain & Tall*, as well as on such series as *Law and Order*, *Wiseguy*, *The Equalizer*, *Spenser for Hire* and *Kate & Allie*.

On stage, Rebhorn appeared in off-Broadway productions like *Life During Wartime*, *I'm Not Rappaport*, *Isn't It Romantic*, *To Gillian on Her 37th Birthday* and as Roderigo in the New York Shakespeare Festival production of *Othello*, besides playing Bernardo in the Circle in the Square production of *Hamlet*.

Brent SPINER
DOCTOR OKUN

Brent Spiner essays the odd, hyperactive scientist Dr Okun, who has been exiled to Area 51 to study the captured spacecraft and its passengers. "Basically, he's been locked in a top-secret room, working on projects for about twenty years," claims Devlin. "So he's a little odd." Spiner was uniquely qualified to play Dr Okun, an expert in all things alien, since he played the android Data on the series *Star Trek: The Next Generation*, as well as in the subsequent movie, *Star Trek: Generations*.

However, Emmerich says that his character was inspired by their *StarGate* special effects supervisor, Jeff Okun: "He had this way of explaining technical terms in interviews that used to crack us up. He'd describe really complicated things using goofy words and we thought it would be fun to have a scientist talk like that." In addition to his idiosyncratic verbal style, Okun possessed a trademark hairdo: long, flowing grey hair. When Spiner heard about this he decided he wanted locks for his character too.

Brent Spiner has also appeared in *Pie in the Sky*, *Miss Firecracker*, opposite Holly Hunter, and Woody Allen's *Stardust Memories*.

On television, Spiner's work includes such movies as the TNT productions of *Huey Long* and *Crazy from the Heart*, both directed by Tom Schlamme, *Sunday in the Park with George*, *Crime of Innocence*, *Robert Kennedy and His Times*, *Manhunt for Claude Dallas*, *The Dain Curse* and *Family Sins*. He has also guest-starred on the television shows *Dream On*, *Mad About You*, *Cheers*, *Night Court* and *Hill Street Blues*. Amongst his stage credits are the Broadway productions of *Big River*, *The Three Musketeers*, *A History of American Film* and *Sunday in the Park with George*. Off-Broadway, Spiner performed in *The Seagull*, *Leave it to Beaver is Dead* and *New Jerusalem*, with the Public Theatre, as well as *Emigrés*, *Table Settings*, *No End of Blame* and, in Los Angeles, *Little Shop of Horrors*, at the Westwood Playhouse. He also toured with the production of *Every Good Boy Deserves Favor*, directed by Patrick Stewart.

Randy QUAID
RUSSELL CASSE

Crop-duster Russell Casse, convinced he's been abducted by aliens and redeposited on Earth, is played with wild-eyed abandon by Randy Quaid. Casse is the character Dean Devlin calls "the Cassandra of the movie."

"Randy Quaid's Russell is a fun character," states Devlin. "He plays a guy who believes that ten years previously he was kidnapped by space aliens. When we started to talk about casting Randy in the role, we began to rewrite it a bit and suddenly the character really began to live. Of course, he took it way beyond anything we could possibly have hoped for. He made it completely unique and original and brought unbelievable humour to it. He represents the common man in the movie. He keeps warning people and nobody listens. Turns out he was right all along.

"More or less this abduction experience ruined his life, because nobody believes his story and they think he is crazy. He gets his revenge though, in the end," Emmerich adds.

Quaid studied drama at the University of Houston, where he met director Peter Bogdanovich, who cast him in *The Last Picture Show*. He went on to appear in three more Bogdanovich films, *Paper Moon*, *What's Up, Doc?* and, twenty years after the original, the sequel to *The Last Picture Show*, *Texasville*. His other film credits include *Days of Thunder*, *Quick Change*, *Parents*, *National Lampoon's Vacation* and *National Lampoon's Christmas Vacation*, *Out Cold*, *The Apprenticeship of Duddy Kravitz*, *Midnight Express*, *Bound for Glory*, *The Missouri Breaks* and *The Long Riders*, which also featured his younger brother Dennis. His portrayal of the kleptomaniac sailor Larry Meadows in *The Last Detail*, with Jack Nicholson, earned Quaid an Academy Award nomination for Best Supporting Actor.

Among Randy Quaid's more recent films are *Kingpin*, opposite Woody Harrelson, the comedy *Bye, Bye Love* and *The Paper*. He also starred in the prison drama *Last Dance*, alongside Sharon Stone and Rob Morrow, and in the Showtime thriller *Woman Undone*, with *Independence Day* co-star Mary McDonnell.

On television, Quaid created a memorable portrait of Lyndon Johnson in the NBC mini-series *LBJ: The Early Years*, for which he won a Golden Globe Award and an Emmy nomination. He garnered a second Emmy nomination for his performance in the ABC production of *A Streetcar Named Desire*. Other mini-series and TV movies include *Frankenstein*, *Inside the Third Reich*, *Of Mice and Men*, *Niagara*, *The Guyana Tragedy*, *Stark Weather: Murder in the Heartland*, *Roommates* and *Next Door*. Quaid also appeared as a series regular on *Saturday Night Live* and starred in the ABC series *Davis Rules*.

His stage credits take in the New York and Los Angeles productions of Sam Shepard's *True West* and the New York Shakespeare in the Park production of *The Golem*.

JAMES DUVAL
LISA JAKUB
JOEY ANDREWS
THE CASSE CHILDREN

Three other young thespians appear in *Independence Day*, playing Russell Casse's children, who, more often than not, parent each other and their ne'er-do-well father. James Duval plays the eldest, Miguel, a teenager forced to shoulder familial responsibilities his father cannot manage.

Lisa Jakub appears as his flirtatious, rebellious sister Alicia and their younger brother Troy is por-

trayed by Guiseppe Andrews. All three were attracted to the film's fantastic science fiction elements as well as the wide arcs their characters experienced.

James Duval, as the steadfast Miguel, made his bow on set astride a motorcycle, speeding down a dusty stretch of Utah road, chasing his errant father, who playfully circled the sky in a beat-up bi-plane. A graduate of several films by independent filmmaker Gregg Araki, Duval displayed an edgy, defiant quality on screen and Emmerich thought this might lend some unpredictable incandescence to Miguel's dependable nature.

James Duval sometimes worked in a Hollywood bar not far from Emmerich's home. The director and his sister Ute, executive producer of *Independence Day*, met Duval there on several occasions to discuss the film with him. As it happened, Duval was a great fan of Emmerich's work.

"I'd seen Roland's other work, including *Moon 44* and *StarGate*... I really think there is something magical about what Roland does. Also, in *Independence Day* there were really moving elements about the human condition that appealed to me. Having worked so much with Gregg Araki, who is a writer-director, I also thought it was great that Roland and Dean wrote the film. That attracts me more than the average script... I think it's more personal when the director is also the writer."

Nonetheless, the scope of *Independence Day* initially overwhelmed Duval, until he began to find certain similarities between Araki's work and *Independence Day*: "It was a tremendous shoot. I was really surprised at how big it was, but what really surprised me was how much every actor was into the film. It was really always about the work, there was no ego involved."

Araki discovered Duval on Melrose Avenue in Los Angeles and cast him in his film, *Totally F**ked Up*. Duval played an innocent, troubled gay youth named Andy in the film and went on to appear in Araki's nihilistic *Doom Generation*, in a role the film-maker wrote for him. Ironically, Duval's third Araki movie, *Nowhere*, featured an alien.

L isa Jakub, whose performance as Robin Williams' oldest daughter in *Mrs Doubtfire* caught the eyes of the film-makers, fancied Alicia's saucy, impertinent attitude, but notes that the alien crisis really "forces her to grow up, to take responsibility for her actions and emotions. That's a powerful concept for her, because her family life has been so scattered." Only seventeen when she lensed her scenes in *Independence Day*, she had been a working actress for thirteen years. "She had the poise and a maturity of someone much older, which was very impressive," Devlin comments. Jakub's additional cinema credits include *A Pig's Tale*, *Matinee*, *Rambling Rose* and *Eleni*. On television, she has appeared in such movies-of-the-week as *Picture Perfect*, *Fight for Justice*, *A Child's Cry for Help*, *The Rape of Dr Willis* and *The Story Lady*. Jakub has also been seen on television series like *Night Court*, *The Twilight Zone*, *Alfred Hitchcock Presents*, *Glory, Glory* and *ER*.

G uiseppe Andrews' portrayal of the resentful youngster Troy was full of surprising nuances. Working closely with Emmerich, Andrews man-

aged to create a character whose naked anger and unabashed pain and hurt were always tempered by a deep ache to right a world that is very wrong.

Andrews has appeared in several movies, including Diane Keaton's critically-acclaimed *Unstrung Heroes*, as well as several independent films. His television credits include guest-starring roles on *Beverly Hills 90210* and *On Our Own*, as well as a starring role in the Fox mini-series *White Dwarf*, produced by Francis Ford Coppola, and the movie-of-the week *12:01*.

Day 2: Attack!

Moon Shadow

Right: *The model department created 'souvenirs' that had been left behind from previous space missions.*

Below: *Erasing the footprints.*

One of the first shots in the movie is an eerie glimpse of the moon, overshadowed by the enormous alien spacecraft travelling towards Earth. In fact, this moonscape was also one of the first effects attempted and, as visual effects supervisor Volker Engel notes, "it was a very tough beginning for us."

The size of the model posed the initial challenge: "It was a such a huge model, it was six metres wide and eight metres deep. This meant that a tremendous amount of light was needed to make it appear as if there was a single light source, representing the sun. We had at least 60,000 watts of light, three big 20ks (key lights) lighting the lunar landscape."

Furthermore, the moon's surface was littered with 'souvenirs' from previous space missions, including an American flag. This flag, as well as the other left-over vanguards, such as a plaque emblazoned with the names of bygone astronauts, were models. However, some were bigger than others, since the visual effects team made ample use of forced perspective.

The script called for footprints embedded in the moon's soft surface, left by visiting astronauts, to be 'erased' by the giant spaceship hovering above. To achieve this, tiny 'footprint stamps', imprinted with the underside of the astronauts' boots, were created. The effects team then stamped several prints along a piece of wood, which was placed on the lunar model and camouflaged to resemble the rest of the surface. A motor attached to this wooden section shook it during shooting so that the footprints etched into the dust magically disappeared.

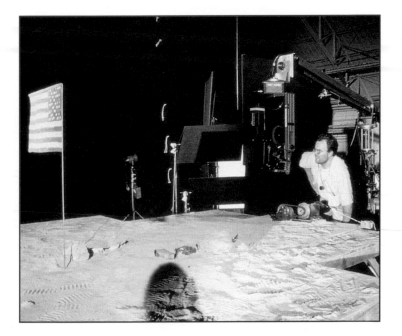

This page: *The visual effects department at work on the moonscape models.*

The Destroyers

T he appearance of the shadow over the Moon heralds the arrival of the Mother Ship and, in turn, the Destroyers she sets loose. The colossal Destroyers, fifteen miles wide, are the deadly ships that justifiably cause worldwide dread. Several incarnations of the Destroyers were born in order to achieve the various shots and effects required.

"Mike Joyce's team built a twelve-foot Destroyer and a thirty-foot Destroyer, which we named the mid-scale Destroyer, and a four-foot Destroyer, which was only used for one shot," Volker Engel says. "We always shot the two first models in different versions, one in which they were placed in a stage full of smoke and one in a clear, smoke-free environment. This technique allowed the compositor to use both versions and dissolve them on top of each other with the percentage of fog that Roland desired. The idea was that we are dealing with a ship that is fifteen miles in diameter and when we look at it from the front, it will appear very crisp. However, if we see a part of the ship that is maybe seven miles away, it will appear more hazy, which was why we used two different versions."

While it was relatively easy to place the twelve-foot Destroyer in a tent full of smoke, the thirty-foot model was more cumbersome. "Basically, it was so big that it had to be built exactly in the place where we were going to shoot it, instead of in the model shop," Mike Joyce recalls.

Below: *A production painting of a Destroyer over Los Angeles.*

Above left: *The highly detailed centrepiece of the twelve-foot Destroyer underbelly (one foot in diameter).*

Below left: *The underbelly of the twelve-foot Destroyer model.*

Far right: *Every Destroyer shot included a separate smoke-pass, so that the right level of haze could be added in post-production.*

Above right: *For the underbelly sections, moulds were made so pieces could be replicated.*

Below right: *Visual effects director of photography, Anna Foerster, takes final measurements for a complex motion control shot at the rim of the Destroyer.*

Above: *The crowd watches the approach of a Destroyer.*

Left: *Another Destroyer casts a shadow over the Eiffel Tower in Paris.*

Above right: *The Schism under the twelve-foot Destroyer measured only three inches. It was only used for wide shots.*

Below right: *For close-ups, a huge mechanical Schism was used.*

Opposite: *To achieve the movement of the petals, the inner doors that reveal the cannon and the cannon itself, five motors were sychronised with every camera move via computer.*

While the awesome size of the Destroyer inspired fear, its most terrifying accoutrement was the Schism, its supremely destructive weapon. The Schism, located in the underbelly of the Destroyers, opens up to disgorge a cannon which fires the devastating beam that annihilates cities around the globe. This spectacular weapon was created entirely via models and computer graphics.

"The diameter of the Schism model was pretty big, about ten feet in diameter and ten feet high," Volker Engel remembers. "It included a very complicated mechanism for opening the petals which reveals the cannon and sticks that come in, representing a sort of time clock to let us know that we are running out of time. We had to film this mechanical masterpiece upside down in order to make it work. It looked like a table with a big opening in it, except that this table was huge and had a constant rotation."

The ungainly Schism proved to be an arduous thing to shoot.

"We had extremely long exposure times. One shot of the Schism took us a day to finish, sometimes, because we had to shoot different passes with smoke, without smoke, a separate light pass, a separate fiber optics pass," Engel explains. "All these passes were later combined in post-production, but each one took between one and four hours of shooting time."

The actual lethal beam was the product of the computer graphics department, which created a magical, malevolent swarm of energy particles, collecting on the exterior and interiors of the Schism model. It formed a beam that became the destruction blast known among the *Independence Day*

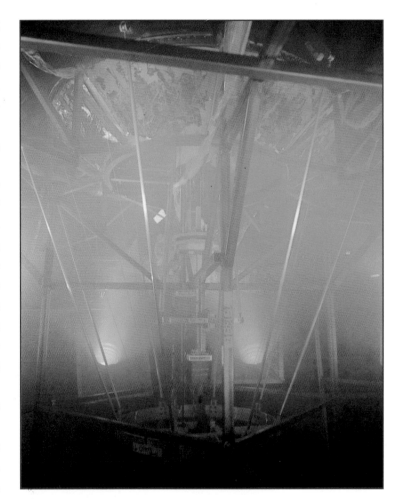

cognoscenti as 'The Hammer'.

While creating this deadly beam, the computer graphics team also had to match the exact conditions in which the model from which it emanated was shot. Specifically, this entailed a blue-green light, already established during photography of the giant model, an atmosphere detailed on Marc Weigert's breakdowns that also had to be encoded into the computer.

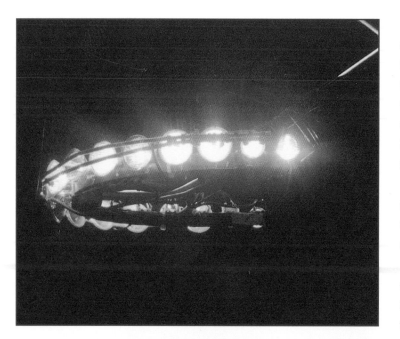

The Phenomenon is an idiosyncratic *Independence Day* effect that first made itself known through the booming voice of the production assistant Lars Winther. Roaring "PHENOMENON," Winther commanded an army of extras from the streets of Manhattan to the Utah deserts to look skyward in horror at this special element that began life in a fish tank in Germany.

Devlin, Emmerich and the effects units envisioned the Phenomenon as an ominous layer of clouds that presaged the advance of one of the aliens' most destructive craft, the Destroyer.

"The Phenomenon was created in a so-called cloud tank, which was really a water tank," Volker Engel explains. "We took the tank that Roland had used in *StarGate* in a scene where James Spader goes

Above and right:
The "Pheno-menon" rig underwater in the cloud tank, consisting of halogen lights and metal piping with tiny holes through which paint was injected into the water.

through the Gate to another world and dimension. We built a system of pipes with holes in them, where we attached lights. Then we put them in water and pumped paint through these very small pipes that were only about a quarter inch thick. The paint spread out in the water and depending on the choreography of the movement of these pipes, the colour would take on different forms. It usually appeared cloudy, which was why we called it a cloud tank.

"The most complex and interesting shot we did with the cloud tank was one in which the audience sees the Destroyer over New York coming out of the Phenomenon cloud. The model department created a shape that looked like the rim of the Destroyer and we instigated the Phenomenon in the cloud tank and pushed this Destroyer rim piece through the cloud."

This effect was eventually combined with the live action footage Emmerich had shot in the early stages of principal photography, when crowds of astonished extras ambled towards a spaceship hovering in the New York sky. The blank heavens towards which they gazed was now filled with an otherworldly danger, thanks to a tank full of dye and clever, state-of-the-art computer compositing.

Above: *A Destroyer swirls out of a "Phenomenon" cloud.*

Global Destruction

Right: *'The End is nigh!'*

Below: *Organising the scenes of confusion in Manhattan.*

The aliens position their Destroyers over most of the world's major cities, ready to wreak incredible havoc. Filming this destruction was obviously a major task, and began in July 1995, at a demolished steel mill in the industrial California city of Fontana. The former Kaiser Steel mill lay in ruins, tall buildings collapsed in heaps, brick and metal scattered about the landscape. The film-makers loved the wreckage and used it to double as the post-alien apocalypse that Los Angeles had become. Unfortunately, this beautiful devastation was about to be cleared away, requiring a hastily rearranged shooting schedule.

"It was a fantastic location, in that there really wasn't much to do to it," Devlin recalls. "It looked like a wave of destruction had just decimated it. We were scheduled to film there a couple of months later, but they wanted to level the whole area to put in a race track. We had to put together a quick pre-shoot to get the location on film."

The *Independence Day* production team descended, adding a few touches, such as traffic lights, stop signs, crashed busses and helicopters, torn billboards and a few valiant palm trees. Burning cars and smoke, pumped in from smoke machines, filled the air with an acrid stench.

"The entire set had to represent different parts of the city and each area had to look like this alien disaster had just hit," Devlin explains. "Because Kaiser Steel had been abandoned for some time, we had to add touches that made it feel like the destruction had happened only minutes before."

Three cameras captured the devastation on film, and while this marked the beginning of the film's principal photography, production, in fact, had begun months before. The model shop, headed by Mike Joyce, commenced crafting miniatures in May 1995. Most of his team's handiwork met a fiery end, the victim of countless explosions, courtesy of the pyro-effects unit. As this volatile but controlled mayhem ensued, mostly in Building 35 at Hughes Aircraft, Devlin, Emmerich and the first unit film crew bombarded Manhattan during a record-breaking heatwave.

Theirs was a five-day blitz, featuring stunts, car crashes, hundreds of extras and several key moments between Judd Hirsch and Jeff Goldblum, who respectively play father and son in the movie.

Because the Manhattan scenes were exteriors,

Above: *Production art detailing the devastation caused by the alien attack.*

Left: *Filming at the abandoned Kaiser Steel works.*

Irwin Allen

The king of the seventies disaster movie was undoubtedly producer Irwin Allen. Allen came to fame in the sixties upon producing a number of highly successful TV series, notably *Voyage to the Bottom of the Sea*, *Lost in Space*, *Time Tunnel* and *Land of the Giants*. He hit paydirt in 1972 when he produced the film that kick-started the seventies disaster movie cycle, *The Poseidon Adventure*. Set on a capsized ocean liner, it featured the now pre-requisite all-star cast: Gene Hackman, Shelley Winters, Ernest Borgnine, Red Buttons, Carol Lynley, Roddy McDowall and Stella Stevens, with the audience on the edge of their seats guessing which cast members would survive. Also featured is Leslie Nielsen, ten years before he successfully spoofed the whole genre in *Airplane!*

Allen followed this success with the even bigger *The Towering Inferno*, featuring an even starrier cast led by Steve McQueen and Paul Newman. Other producers quickly got in on the act with, amongst others, *Earthquake*, the *Airport* series and *The Hindenburg* following in rapid succession.

He continued producing disaster movies into the early eighties, but Allen's Midas touch seemed to have deserted him by the time he revisited the scene of his greatest success with *Beyond the Poseidon Adventure* and then teamed with Paul Newman again for the prophetically titled *When Time Ran Out*.

Irwin Allen finally passed away in 1991, but his tradition is kept very much alive by Roland Emmerich's and Dean Devlin's all-star approach to *Independence Day* ■

Right: *Extras observe the arrival of a Destroyer above the streets of New York.*

Opposite above: *Another amazing stunt as Boomer leaps to safety.*

Opposite below: *Filming more of the alien attack aftermath, a scene that was cut from the final print.*

filming began early, to utilise as much daylight as possible. Unfortunately, the punishing heat simmered just as early; ninety degrees by 6am, and climbing in tandem with suffocating humidity. The production visited a broad swath of the city and its environs, from Wall Street to SoHo to beneath the Manhattan Bridge, ending the sojourn across the river in a bucolic New Jersey park and a nearby hillside neighbourhood of sturdy brownstone homes, with the enthusiastic residents recruited as extras.

The initial scenes called for an army of extras, filmed in various stages of reaction to the appearance of the alien ships. The first day of shooting, underneath the Manhattan Bridge, had fifty or so extras wandering like zombies towards the water, looking skyward, mouths gaping at the underbelly of a huge spaceship and the ominous shadow it cast. Of course, all they saw was blue sky and a camera crew. The ship and its shadow would be added later in post-production, although the first assistant director

Right: *Roland Emmerich talks the actors through an important scene.*

Below: *Jeff Goldblum negotiates his bike through the carefully choreographed car crashes.*

Sergio Mimica-Gezzan tried to provide a focal point for several young thespians, whose basketball game is interrupted by the looming shadow of the spaceship. Waving a bottle of water aloft, he exhorted them to "look at the ship" and the ballplayers complied, staring at the universe's most potable space craft. The shadow appeared, courtesy of a strange rig, a large black flag attached to a short truss, sitting on top of a dolly that moved it backwards and forwards.

Emmerich also set up five cameras that morning, to capture the hapless New York cabbies and drivers on their way to work as they crashed into each other, their eyes naturally focused above. These supposed native New Yorkers were actually trained stunt drivers, and Emmerich and stunt coordinator Dan Brad-

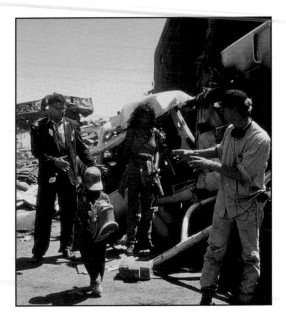

ley carefully choreographed their 'accidents.'

In the coming days, the crowd and the pandemonium increased exponentially. Early on Saturday morning, before the tourists and shoppers arrived, 300 extras filled the streets of SoHo and, on Emmerich's cue, ran for their lives, in desperate attempts to escape the alien force. More flying cars and stupendous crashes were filmed, featuring sixteen cars in all and including an airborne truck that slammed into the side of a police car. The frenzy moved to Wall Street, although the fleeing extras and rampant hysteria didn't seem to concern the local businessmen and women, who, after all, were accustomed to their own crashes and panic.

One of the most memorable crowd scenes included 300 extras, all desperately attempting to flee the city while Jeff Goldblum effectively manoeuvres through the chaos on his bicycle. This elab-

This page: *The vision of a ruined LA becomes a reality.*

Above: *One of the many impressive finished explosions seen in the film.*

orate undertaking called for meticulously placed cars, in bumper-to-bumper gridlock, horns blaring, smashing into each other at rehearsed moments, just missing Goldblum as he negotiated his bicycle through the mêlée. At the same time, people were screaming and running, carrying as many of their possessions as possible or tossing their belongings to waiting cars from tenement windows, with clothes and boxes flying through the air. Of course,

it took some time to set this shot up, an army of assistant directors and production assistants positioning cars and directing extras as Goldblum rehearsed his route through the traffic for Emmerich. As everything approached readiness, Emmerich paced and Devlin circled, a cellular phone affixed to his ear. The shot was delayed. It seemed the camera, on its way from a prior location, had got stuck in a real Manhattan traffic jam.

During this time, a streamlined second unit team, headed by associate producer Peter Winther, shot various aspects of the city, from the Empire State Building to a postcard panorama of Manhattan. Such shots were specifically designed for later effects, which would be inserted into this 'plate shot.' The first unit team would often divide and multiply into various splinter crews, as filming required, alternately headed by Winther or Devlin. After Winther's troop completed its duties in New York, they winged their way to Washington DC, to lens equivalent shots there.

By mid-August, the company had moved to Los Angeles, where principal photography would be

completed. The production made a grand entrance. The first scheduled scene required the rooftops of ten buildings in downtown Los Angeles. Each roof held a crowd of enthusiastic sign-waving extras, playing UFO believers welcoming the alien presence above. A camera was placed on each roof, to film the exuberant extras, and helicopters bearing cameras shot the event from above. Ultimately, Emmerich would also add the sinister canopy of the looming spacecraft to the sky.

The shot took ten days to pre-rig and had to be completed by the end of the magic hour just before dark. Assistant directors Sergio Mimica-Gezzan and Kim Winther organised the event. Fifty extras per roof plus twenty-one stunt players were coordinated, dispatched to the wardrobe, hair and make-up departments, posted to their proper buildings and rehearsed. A small team of camera operators, grips and electricians positioned cameras and lights on

Above: *Filming on the rooftops as Los Angeles welcomes the aliens.*

Left: *Actress Kiersten Warren during the same scene.*

each roof and since Emmerich couldn't be present physically on each building, he supervised the entire operation via walkie-talkie and video. As the sun began to set over the twinkling lights of Los Angeles, cameras rolled and the shot proceeded flawlessly. The swooping choppers caused a minor traffic jam, however, as workers on their way home that Friday night slowed their cars on the freeway to gaze at this odd dance in the sky.

These downtown buildings reappeared in miniature at Hughes Aircraft, where the production completed most of the remaining principal photography. Despite the warm welcome the sign-bearing UFO believers offered, the alien force would blast them into eternity, obliterating Los Angeles in the process. Equal opportunity destroyers, they also wiped out Washington DC, New York, Houston and a host of international cities, from Moscow to Sydney. Each city responded to the alien visitors in completely different ways.

"It was fun to film how different cities might react to the aliens," Devlin says. "In New York and Washington DC, they immediately start to panic and evacuate. Of course, in Los Angeles, people go up on the roof with big billboards, saying 'Welcome home'." Not surprisingly, the majority of 'contactee claims' come from California, so the sign-waving scene was actually quite appropriate.

The production travelled to several locations while in Los Angeles, including the famed Biltmore Hotel, where the first Oscar ceremonies were held. On the steps overlooking a courtly lounge, Mary McDonnell, as The First Lady, addressed the press and the nation. Her eloquent speech, laced with quiet bravery, contrasted with the blatant blare of the helicopter she later boarded, also shot on the roof of the hotel that same night.

Other Los Angeles locales included the freeway adjacent to Los Angeles Airport (LAX), which the production transformed into a multitude of people and cars, trying to escape Manhattan. An endless parade of extras fled into the night, scurrying down a thin ribbon of grass alongside a stream of methodically arranged vehicles. The camera captured the chaos from a bridge above. Later that night, the production staged another traffic jam, this one to accommodate a precarious stunt in which David and Julius, in a desperate race to Washington DC, drive Julius' dilapidated car against traffic, swerving and fishtailing before jumping into the appropriate lane.

Fittingly, Emmerich and company ended principal photography with a genuine bang. The comp-

Below: *Scenes of cars fleeing the city needed careful co-ordination.*

Left: *Vivica A. Fox and Ross Bagley emerge from the wreckage.*

Below: *Roland Emmerich surveys the damage.*

any camped out in downtown Los Angeles, filming more traffic jams and general panic scenes as Angelenos, just like their Manhattan counterparts, looked skyward in horror. At 6am, as the sun peaked over the skyscrapers, three 'buildings', specially built and rigged to the rafters with Clay Pinney's explosives, burst into flames, as the stunt team, padded and covered with protective gel, leapt and scattered, pummelled by the force of the blast. More victims of alien scorching. These live action sequences were then composited into the overall destruction of Los Angeles, the first scenes shot in the movie, during post-production.

Creating Destruction

Right: *The Statue of Liberty model was shot in the parking lot in front of a real sky. Model-maker, Chris Simmons, bolts the pedestal to the table to avoid any shaking during the shot.*

The destruction resulting from the Destroyers' attack is immense as they reduce Los Angeles, Washington, New York, Paris *et al* to rubble. Such widescale annihilation naturally required the cooperation of the production's model-making department, which was led by Mike Joyce. Joyce had previously worked on *Batman Forever*, amongst many others, but even he was slightly taken back by the number of models required for *Independence Day*.

"After I read the script for the first time and we

did a breakdown of the miniatures, I realised that there were more of them needed in this movie than probably any two movies combined. There were spaceships of all kinds, cities to build, aircraft, monuments... the whole gamut of just about everything you could do in movies."

During production, Mike Joyce had a large number of people working for him. Their creations, Joyce notes, began as an idea generated by Emmerich and his design team, Oliver Scholl and Patrick Tatopoulos. While some of the well-known icons were obvious, eventually many of the other models they would create were standardised once their look was established.

"By the time it got to me, it was pretty well set

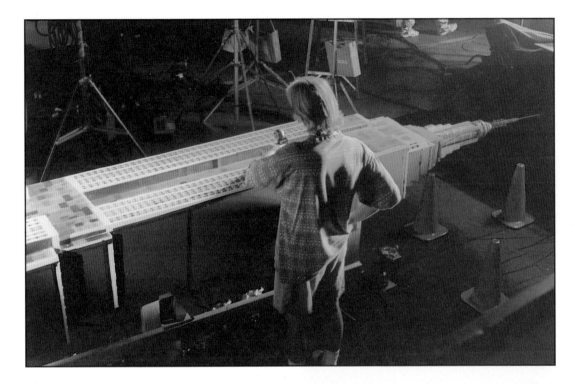

Left: *Gaffer, Victor Abbene, taking light meter readings against the model of the Empire State Building.*

Opposite bottom: *The Lincoln memorial model, carved out of foam, was only two and a half feet tall.*

Below: *The five-foot, detailed White House model.*

how they wanted it designed and built," states Joyce. "Depending on how intricate it was, they would sometimes tell me how much detail they wanted in drawings." The models the department produced from these drawings became the template for everything else: for "our lighting, our paint jobs, our mounts for motion control."

The model department had to replicate several landmarks, including "the White House, one of our main pieces, the Capitol Building, the Washington Monument and the Lincoln Memorial."

While the models represented only a portion of the effects shots, they did enable Emmerich to shoot a good deal of them 'in-camera', such as the fireball.

"Emmerich knows how to use miniatures, how

Above left and right: *The stage is smoked in and the explosion is triggered.*

Above right: *Model-maker, Alan Faucher, adds the last details to the Manhattan miniature.*

to photograph them," Joyce says. He adds that for the type of shots required in *Independence Day*, "miniatures work best. A lot of explosions, a lot of pyro, lots of fires — elements that, even today, with sophisticated computers, are still tricky to do."

Exploding cities were another common feature, a combustible collaboration between the model department and the pyro-effects unit. Mike Joyce's model-makers would craft intricate reproductions of everything from downtown Los Angeles' First Interstate Building to the Statue of Liberty, from the Empire State Building to the White House. Emmerich accomplished most of his explosions using an 'in-camera' method of actually exploding the models, as opposed to achieving the effect via computer.

"There are certain things that a model is very good for. When you blow up a big model, there is nothing better than that on film," Emmerich says. "You can't create that with CGI (computer generated images) yet. Fire, for instance, is very bad in CGI because it is

Left: *The first fireballs were triggered behind the model shop. A street with two rows of buildings was represented by wooden boxes mounted on a piece of plywood. The set-up was tilted in a ninety degree angle with the camera mounted on top. The fireball rises up, and on film we see it crawling down the street towards the camera.*

so random and unpredictable. I think old-fashioned effects, like models, will never die out because they're simply too good for certain things, like explosions. A computer can't make a building explode in the same way that real explosives do, at least not yet."

The aliens' favoured method of devastation was something the film-makers dubbed the 'wall of destruction,' where a massive column of fire engulfs the cities from the sky. Therefore, the model depart-ment built miniatures of New York and Los Angeles neighbourhoods, in various scales, to accommodate different shots. The models required an incredible amount of detail, in order to convince the audience

that the aliens had just destroyed an actual city, not just a model. For instance, the generic Los Angeles street, Mike Joyce recounts, "was about eight feet wide and twenty feet long and included the buildings, all the lighting, the signs and billboards, telephone poles, street lights, parking meters. Everything a city street would have."

Joyce also constructed model interior sets, for close-up views of various settings during the demolition. For example, his artisans crafted an interior office. "The scale was larger because the shot was closer to it," Joyce explains. "It included desks, the computers, telephones, chairs, the coffee makers, fax machines, everything in miniature."

This page and opposite: *Models used for street scenes.*

Above: *The wall of flame seen over a model.*

Eventually, these amazing creations made their way over to Joe Viskocil's pyro-effects team, under the guidance of visual effects supervisor Volker Engel, where they would become victims of the 'wall of destruction.' For the most part, this awesome annihilation occurred in Building 35 at Hughes Aircraft. After a bit of trial and error, the method of choice was as follows: the pyro and visual effects departments positioned the models at a specific angle and set a remote-controlled camera, shooting at high speed, in a scaffold nicknamed The Magic Carpet, perched near the ceiling, swathing the camera in flame-retardant material. Viskocil ignited the fireball below the model. Flames shot up towards camera, over the rooftops of the model cities, filling the room with a giant, orange blaze. Because of the way the models were angled and the natural tendency of fire to travel upwards, it appeared as if a terrible wall of flame had rolled over New York and Los Angeles.

The high speed film allowed Emmerich to slow down its horrible path, in sync with the standard twenty-four frames per second film.

"It's basically a chimney effect," Emmerich explains. "Fire always wants to go up, so all we had to do was build streets and objects upright. The street became sort of a chimney for the fire. We're not the first ones to do that, but we did it on a bigger scale."

They employed the 'chimney effect' against the advice of many special effects experts.

"When we came up with this fireball coming down the Manhattan Street, every effects person we talked to said, 'Be prepared for a $150,000 shot'," Devlin recalls. "We said, 'Well, why is this so difficult to do?' and they said, 'Because not only do you have to shoot the street and shoot all the elements of the street, but you'll have to digitally composite them into your shot and that will be very expensive.' Roland said, 'Well, why can't we just do it all in-camera?' Everyone said it wouldn't work or it would look fake. So, Roland came up with this idea of building the street in miniature, putting it on a platform, standing it on end and placing the camera on top and the fire below. Everyone said, 'Eeeh, I don't know if it will work.' Well, it worked spectacularly and a $150,000 shot became a $30,000 shot."

Devlin goes on to note that this creative, problem-solving approach is one of Emmerich's strengths as a film-maker: "Roland is not about throwing money at the most expensive shot or using the newest toy invented. It's about the most creative solution to a problem. Roland is incredible at inventing new ways of doing shots."

Above left: *The 'Los Angeles street' is prepped by the pyro crew.*

Below left: *This eight foot by twelve foot tabletop of a destroyed Los Angeles was enhanced in post-production with fires and explosions (shot as separate elements) and computer-generated F-18s.*

This page: *Ten-inch model cars are lifted off a wire mesh street with air-cannons. The bluescreen is replaced by the exploding Empire State Building in post-production.*

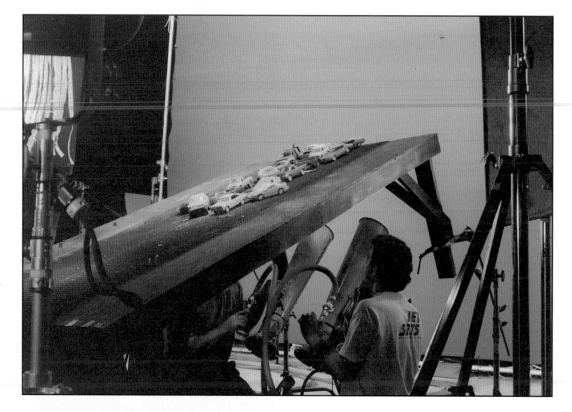

This page: *Visual effects production supervisor, Bob Hurrie, and key grip, David Novak, crash a four-foot model of a bus through a StarGate billboard. A ninety-degree tilted camera, a lot of additional debris and Fuller's earth were needed to make this shot work, although it was finally cut from the film.*

The White House

Opposite above: *Last preparations before the big explosion.*

Below: *A close-up of the model White House steps.*

Perhaps the most notable landmark the aliens destroy is The White House. The production team were fortunate that Castle Rock had recently built an exact scale version of the White House rooms for *The American President*. Oliver Stone used it afterwards in *Nixon*, and *Independence Day* inherited it next. The Oval Office, the Press Briefing Room, even the President's bedroom and breakfast room appeared on the Hughes lot. Wearing regulation Presidential cufflinks, Pullman conducted interviews on behalf of *Independence Day* on the White House 'lawn', a small patch of astro-turf surrounding the set.

To film the evacuation of the White House, the company took a night trip to the high desert in Santa Clarita. Portions of the White House materialised in a grassy field, with the President, his daughter, his governmental entourage and David and Julius Levinson hastily exiting the stately building to board the waiting Presidential helicopter. A giant green, regulation chopper waited outside the famous edifice, but the set was mostly facade, all painted flats, wallpapered plywood and corridors leading nowhere. The scene would later piece together with the White House explosion; as the helicopter, loaded with its pivotal passengers, took off, the White House would erupt. Fortunately, the clever use of the exploding model White House meant that demolition experts were not required to destroy the set at three in the morning.

The model was an exceptional creation, the model department's showpiece. It stood five feet high and sat on a bluff near Hughes Aircraft for awhile before its destruction. The model was so detailed and authentic that the film-makers decided to use it for a few forced perspective shots, whereby the model is placed a short distance away in relation to the camera, so it appears as though it is far away. Extras 'protesting' the government's handling of the alien crisis marched in front of a real fence placed in front of the model, set back 100 feet in the distance.

Like most of the other models, however, the White House met a violent end. Pyrotechnics supervisor Joe Viskocil fixed thirty to forty explosive charges at key points about the model and nine cameras, filming at high speeds, captured the event. The model itself was decorated with dollhouse sized furniture so that the debris bursting forth would appear as real objects.

Below left: *The explosion.*

Below right: *The aftermath: only the metal structure is still standing.*

Over: *The spectacular finished result.*

The Aliens

Right: *A production sketch of the biomechanical alien torso.*

Below: *Dr Okun is trapped with the captured alien.*

The invading aliens that cause this wide-spread destruction were envisioned by Roland Emmerich as creatures that are both familiar and completely original, in terms of their demeanour and configuration. Emmerich worked closely with production designer Patrick Tatopoulos on their design in order to achieve this tricky combination.

"I wanted them to follow the mythology of what people expect aliens to look like, to some extent," Emmerich explains. "There's a certain kind of popular image that everybody constantly draws and I

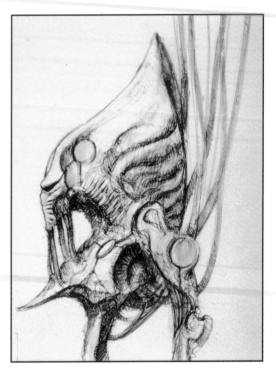

wanted to stick with that. But, on the other hand, I thought, that's terribly boring. So, we kind of used both those ideas. The first image of the alien is not what you think they typically look like. You later discover, in a surprise, that they're exactly how we think they should appear. We simply disguised them first and then slowly revealed their true appearance."

To make these dual images work, Tatopoulos conceived an entire history and evolution of the alien population.

"We had to come up with something, in terms of a backstory. A reason why those aliens are like that, why they move the way they do, why they act certain ways," Tatopoulos says. "After we established that, it was easier to create them and their space-

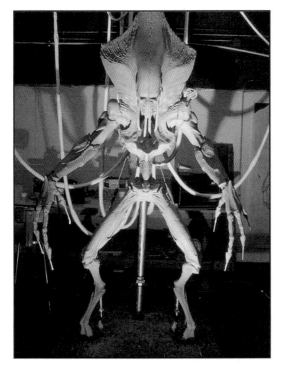

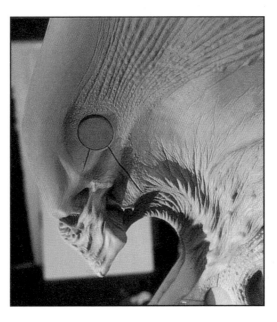

ships, because we knew how they lived."

"The thing that made the creatures in *Alien* and *Predator* so compelling is that there was such a clear system about how they behaved and acted," Devlin notes. "The audience didn't need an enormous explanation to understand them and be frightened of them. The trick was to create a new system and I believe Patrick Tatopoulos and Oliver Scholl came up with one that works enormously well."

Devlin adds that although the aliens intend to take over our planet, they are not motivated by hate.

"The aliens are ambivalent about us. They're like a force of nature, like locusts that show up and destroy a farmer's crops. They aren't good or bad, they are simply a race that moves from planet to

Above left: *The full size alien model.*

Above right: *The biomechanical alien hands.*

Left: *The model mock-up of the biomechanical alien head.*

Right: *Model of the little rod-puppet alien.*

Below left: *The biomechanical suit.*

Below right: *Legs for the biomechanical suit.*

planet consuming resources: water, food, air. And we're the next stop. Human beings are like bugs to them, mild annoyances, and they just want us exterminated. They just want us out of the way. They're the new tenants and they're moving in."

Unlike many science fiction movies, the actors actually got a glimpse of their enemies, albeit in puppet form. In fact, for a while, a small film team, fondly referred to as 'The Tentacle Unit', devoted its time and resources solely to filming these creatures.

"Roland likes to do as much as possible in front of the camera and computer technology and animation isn't really advanced enough yet to capture

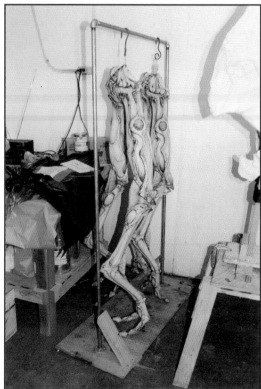

Left and below left: *At work on the alien model.*

Below right: *A biomechanical alien hand, after the highly detailed paint job.*

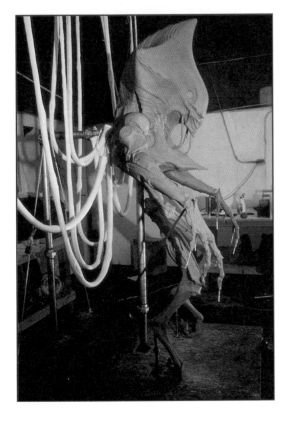

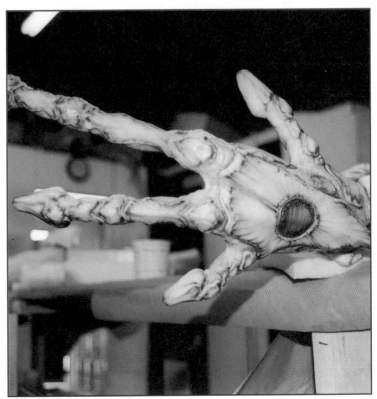

Right: *Director, Roland Emmerich, demonstrates how he wants the movement of the alien's legs.*

Below: *The captured alien communicates through Dr Okun.*

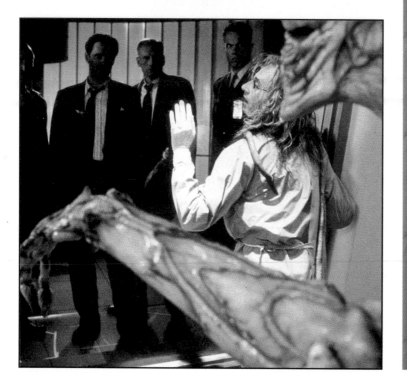

Close Encounters

The disbelief faced by Russell Casse when he relates his story is a common experience for alleged victims of alien abduction. Nevertheless, there are many documented cases, also known as Close Encounters of the Fourth Kind, from all parts of the world and many of them feature strikingly similar characteristics.

The abductee will often tell of being strangely transported from an isolated location, frequently to a spaceship. Here the victim will usually undergo some kind of an examination, nearly always medical and frequently sexual in nature. This may then be followed by a tour round the spaceship, and some form of communication also tends to be involved, although this is mainly non-verbal.

Are aliens conducting some strange kind of medical experiments on the human race? That is at least one suggestion that's been put forward, known as the Alien Genetic Testing Theory. However, others believe alien visitors have more benign intentions, that extraterrestrials have overseen the development of the planet, on occasion even pointing the human race in the right direction.

Not surprisingly, those involved are often reluctant to talk of their experiences. In fact, many are only aware of a missing period of time and actually can't describe what has happened to them. One of the earliest and best known cases is that of American couple Betty and Barney Hill, who sighted a spacecraft and experienced 'missing time' whilst driving through New Hampshire in 1961. However, they were unable to remember anything of their abduction until they submitted to hypnosis. It was only in 1964 that they actually came forward, relating their encounter and prompting many other people to also tell their remarkably similar tales. ■

the kinds of movements and looks we wanted for our creatures," notes Tatopoulos. "I didn't really want to design the alien so that it could sustain a living person inside, because that's what it would end up looking like; a man in a suit. For that reason, we used a lot of different techniques. We did make an alien torso and arms worn by a puppeteer for the shots where the legs weren't seen, but we made separate mechanical legs and a full-sized creature, about eight feet tall, with twenty-five feet long tentacles, which was all cabled and radio-controlled. For scenes that required the aliens to run and do more refined and precise movements, we used rod puppets, which were about a foot and a half long. We also created a mechanical head, which we placed on a special harness."

Tatopoulos chose silicone as the basis for his aliens, as opposed to the customary foam latex. "Silicone gives a much more interesting transparency effect, you can read the layers much better and it gives it a glossy look, which I find very interesting." Even the aliens found it difficult to retain their watery sheen in the Wendover desert, however. Tatopoulos and his technicians came prepared with a special solution to maintain their slithery surface and, in between takes, they sprayed the parched creatures with a fine mist of K-Y jelly.

The difference between the *Independence Day* aliens and previous cinematic extraterrestrials was not merely skin deep. These visitors had their own, singular agenda.

Left: *General Grey confronts the captured alien.*

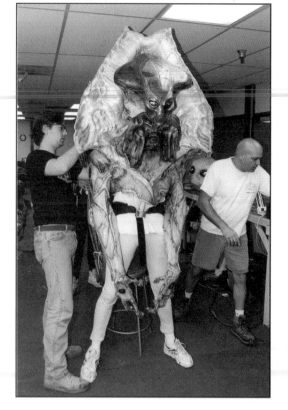

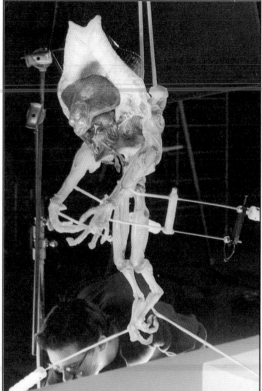

Far left: *The creature effects crew prepping the alien for a costume test for the lab sequence.*

Below: *Creature supervisor, Patrick Tatopoulos, preparing the biomechanical suit for the skull-splitting scene.*

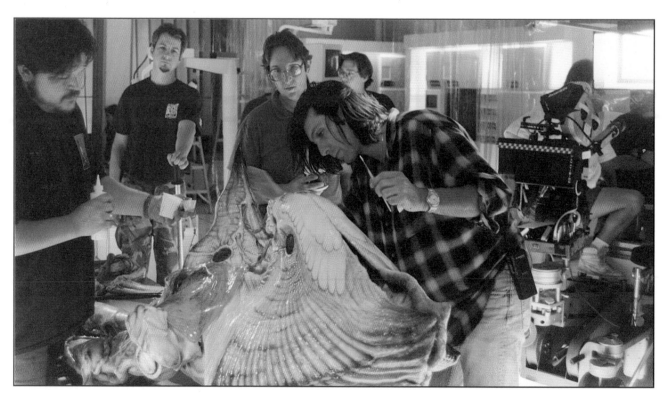

"One of the things we haven't seen a lot of in these types of films is an attack," Devlin points out. "I think that *War of the Worlds* was probably the only one that really explored that. For the most part, in alien invasion movies, they come down to Earth and they're hidden in some back field. Only some guy in the mountains, you know, in No Wheresville, sees them and no one believes him. Or they arrive in little spores and they inject themselves into the back of someone's head. When we started writing this, Roland said to me, 'If you could travel nine billion light years across the galaxy, would you hide on the farm or would you make a big entrance?' We decided our aliens would make a big entrance."

Opposite above left *The finished rod-puppet alien. The green rods were removed in postproduction and the green background was replaced with live-action shots of the lab.*

This page: *The remains of the captured Area 51 aliens.*

Day 3: Action!

Area 51

Right: *Model-maker, Jason Kaufman, adds the finishing touches to the interior of the Area 51 underground hangar model.*

President Whitmore discovers from the ex-director of the CIA, Albert Nimziki, that recovered alien bodies have been kept hidden in Area 51 for many years. The production shot the exteriors for Area 51 at Wendover Airport. With its combination of forties-period boxy hangars and squat, square buildings, Wendover Airport proved a fortuitous architectural find and its airstrip was extremely well-suited to double for the infamous military site.

Reputedly, Area 51 is a special section at a top-secret military testing site in the Nevada desert.

Situated near a dry lake bed called Groom Lake, Area 51, or Dreamland as it is also known, has historically hosted several covert military operations; U2 pilots trained there in the 1950s and subsequent state-of-the-art aerospace technology, including the Stealth bomber, various Star Wars mechanisms and assorted supersonic spy planes, were supposedly researched and developed there. Students of Area 51 speculate that the government also studied alien technology there, via crashed spaceships, recovered and spirited to the secret base. The government steadfastly denies the existence of Area 51 and/or any clandestine programmes involving the study of alien craft.

"Area 51 was supposed to have been built in the late fifties or early sixties," Devlin explains. "The

This page:
Various produc-
tion sketches
show both the
exterior and
interior of
Area 51.

Opposite below:
Bill Pullman, as
President Whit-
more, comes face
to face with the
recovered alien
bodies.

Area 51

Everything about Area 51 is shrouded in secrecy. In fact, it is so secret that even the government denies its existence. To be found just under 100 miles north of Las Vegas, there are numerous warning signs and devices to further discourage any potentially inquisitive visitors.

Over the years, many highly secret projects have been tested at Area 51, also known as 'Dreamland', 'Skunk Works' or 'The Ranch'. The U2 spy plane and the Stealth bomber, both tested here, are just two of the more famous examples. It is also widely believed that Area 51 contains evidence of visitors from outer space, in particular the remains of the UFO and aliens from Roswell.

Roswell is the stuff of UFO legend. On 2 July 1947, something crashed during the night in Corona, New Mexico and was later taken to the Roswell Army airfield. Here it was announced that the military had actually recovered the remains of a crashed flying saucer, although this claim was later retracted and the UFO identified as a weather balloon. This was strenuously denied by the initial witnesses, but was also rapidly followed by a general clamp down on the story. However, in 1994 the government admitted the remains had indeed been changed, in order to cover-up a top secret test they were conducting during the early years of the Cold War. Roswell remained hot news a year later when Ray Santilli acquired film footage taken by an ex-Army cameraman which allegedly showed an autopsy being performed on one of the aliens from the flying saucer. It would be very surprising if we had heard the last of Roswell. ■

buildings and design of the hangars at Wendover Airport were much more reminiscent of the architecture of that period than any modern air force bases, so we thought it would be a pretty good match for the exteriors of Area 51."

The interior of Area 51 that leads to a giant lab which housed the captured spaceship, was built at the Hughes facility. Since the government denies the existence of Area 51, production designers Oliver Scholl and Patrick Tatopoulos enjoyed a great deal of creative latitude in inventing their version of the enigmatic installation. They decided that, since it is a secret place, it would be underground and very clinical in both look and feel, a combination of science and the military. The result was a long, narrow corridor, lined with opaque green glass panels and embedded lights. Computers and fragments of spaceships were the only decoration. The white ramp in the centre of the hallway angled up at the end, towards a broad window, which revealed a bunker

Below: *A foam-core mock-up of the Area 51 underground hangar model was built by the model shop to get an impression of how big the model had to be. It was built twice the size of the mock-up.*

Left: *The research lab housing the captured alien space ship.*

Below: *Oliver Scholl incorporated the 'R' and '2' as a homage to Star Wars.*

that contained a leviathan spaceship. This captured Attacker represented one of the aliens' smallest ships, but it was the biggest 'model' built for the film, about sixty-five feet wide. It literally filled an aeroplane hangar, which had been transformed by the art and construction departments into a forbidding and austere research facility. Its 'concrete' facade was achieved by a clever use of plaster, wood and sand.

"The set was really designed around the spaceship," Scholl explains. "We tried to create a clean, structural, architectural look with strong, straight geometric lines. This would contrast with the spaceship, which was very organic in shape, very fluid and

detailed, almost a living thing. Roland wanted to have these ramps connecting the long hallway set and the set that housed the spaceship. We knew that the reveal of the spaceship would be from a higher position, at the top of the ramp, so the whole set and the spaceship's position were laid out for that shot. The hangar that contained the ship was, basically, a research lab, but we designed it to enhance the appearance of the ship and support the underground feeling of Area 51. The main walls were tilted forward, to emphasise the weight above, and we added hard, angled columns, to augment that feeling of something from above pushing down on the place. We also added horizontal divisions to the side walls, to direct the focus to the spaceship, and big windows to the side, in which other activity could be going on, to show the scale of the facility."

Above: *Production designers Scholl and Tatopoulos decided on a clinical look to the set.*

Right: *The finished Area 51 'clean room' set before shooting.*

Scholl, who began his career in industrial design, did manage to have a little fun with the stark interior of Area 51. On one side of the ramp overlooking the spaceship, he painted a mysterious, large blue 'R' with a '2' on the other side, a nod to the famous R2-D2 droid from the *Star Wars* series.

Director of photography Karl Walter Lindenlaub, in his sixth collaboration with Emmerich, worked with the lighting department to highlight the astonishing creation.

The geography of the set, with its smooth floors, high ceilings and ramps, accommodated a variety of camerawork, from dolly shots to Steadicam to a sweeping crane manoeuvre with a camera remote. It also enabled Lindenlaub to experiment with colour, specifically with special lights called 'cyberlights'.

"Cyberlights are often used in rock 'n' roll con-certs and work with a beam splitter and a mirror to drop out certain rays from the spectrum while letting other ones through, creating different colours and also various patterns. One light unit could make any colour we wanted and we could programme that colour and the light changes into a computer."

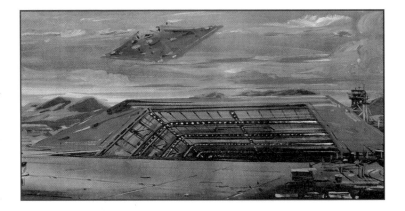

Above: *A production sketch showing the Attacker leaving its bunker.*

Left: *Another view of the research lab.*

The Attacker

Right: *The early stages of an Attacker model.*

Below: *A design sketch showing the captured Attacker.*

Also housed deep in Area 51 was a captured Attacker. This Attacker spaceship was, as production designer Patrick Tatopoulos points out, "a huge undertaking, not just because of its size. This thing had to be a practical set. Area 51 workers were supposed to walk on it. Actors were supposed to stand in the cockpit and we had to put cameras inside to shoot the cockpit itself. So, the whole thing had to be a heavy structure. We did a lot of soldering and welding to make it very rigid. It wasn't like a traditional set where you would usually use

plywood. It was a full metal construction."

The spaceship started life as a simple drawing, as Mike Joyce, head of the model department, explains: "The Attacker spaceship began as drawings that we had to translate three-dimensionally. We built a twenty-four inch Attacker out of clay to get the basic shape. Once we got that, a sculptor made it out of foam. We made a mould of it and came up with a hard shell and used that to put all the fine detail on it. When that was done, we moulded that and produced a part."

Cinematographer Karl Walter Lindenlaub and his crew also played a vital role in the realisation of the Attacker. They assayed several patterns and colours, discarding most of the former, which "seemed to look too much like disco lighting." Lindenlaub finally settled on a deep, steel-blue colour for the ship's top, with some green touches below.

These colours played into Tatopoulos' overall conception of the spaceship and the aliens who designed it. Tatopoulos, whose background is

Left: *The finished Attacker during the live-action shoot.*

Below: *Roland Emmerich and property master Douglas Harlocker with the Attacker.*

make-up design and creature effects, also designed the creature in Emmerich's *StarGate* and took on the same assignment in *Independence Day*. He thought the ship would be an extension of the aliens' world, uniquely suited to their needs and tastes. The natural look of the craft, so antithetical to the Spartan, clean interior Area 51, sprang directly from Tatopoulos' vision of the alien world. He likens the ship's structure to that of a thick, ornate oyster shell that provides transportation, protection and shelter. This architecture, he explains, reflects the aliens' physical configuration, as well as their very civilisation.

"Patrick is very into organic forms and I think this was his big contribution to the film," Emmerich comments. "He established this alien culture as something living and organic, but not like anything that we could identify as humans. He made it believable and alien to us at the same time. Oliver (Scholl), on the other hand, is very good in techni-

cal things, which are more human, in a way. We're more used to technology. So, the two looks were kind of contradicting and balancing each other out in the movie, which is very good."

In the Desert

Right: *Roland Emmerich on location.*

Below and opposite: *Filming on the desolate Salt Flats.*

Following the aliens' overwhelming attack, a convoy of vehicles and travellers converge on Area 51. These scenes were filmed at Wendover, a border town straddling Utah and Nevada, which is mostly a desert, bisected by a strip of the I-80 highway. However, Wendover is most famous for two locations, both of which *Independence Day* visited: the Wendover Airport, the one-time home of the *Enola Gay*, and the Bonneville Salt Flats.

The Salt Flats consist of about 45,000 acres of

crystalline salt, the remains of the ancient Lake Bonneville. This expanse of salt and sky has since become the renowned Bonneville Speedway and during 'Speed Week' hundreds of cars and motorcycles journey to Wendover, hoping to break the world-record speeds routinely set there.

While the cast and crew of *Independence Day* didn't set any speed records, they certainly established a standard for endurance. The miles of alabaster salt and endless azure sky provided a stark backdrop for an alien arrival, its broad scope especially suited to the wide Super 35 frame Emmerich and cinematographer Karl Walter Lindenlaub favoured. Unfortunately, it definitely did not offer any shade or relief from the pounding desert heat. To make matters worse, the salt was not particularly hospitable to tires, cables, shoes and eyes.

"The salt basically ate through everything," Devlin recalls. "The longer we had equipment there, the more it got destroyed. All the cables and tires constantly kept popping. And it was about 126 degrees in the sun. Plus, it is an area known for high winds and bizarre salt storms, which we experienced first-hand. We were shooting one day and it was beautiful blue skies, no clouds. We thought, oh, we're going to have a terrific day. All of a sudden, way off in the distance, we saw this smoky pillar. We didn't know what it was, but within fifteen minutes we were in the centre of a giant salt storm. We had to shut down for a couple hours, but made it up that afternoon."

Despite these unique problems, Devlin adds that the Salt Flats and the surrounding desert also provided the perfect setting for the film: "The Salt Flats were an amazing landscape, because the salt and sky sometimes melted into the horizon. And since the salt is so white, very different lighting effects happen. There is something other-worldly about it. We thought it would bring the audience somewhere they hadn't been to before."

The vast, pristine horizon, unmarred by buildings or power lines, offered the perfect palette in which to add in subsequent effects. This eerie plain of salt also served as a bizarre stage, across which a tired, angry Captain Steven Hiller hauls a captive alien, the misguided creature who had the gall to take on the gifted Captain in a sky-high dogfight. Hiller, a cocky, talented Marine fighter pilot, was played with aplomb by Will Smith. Screaming very personal, unscripted epithets at the unearthly POW he dragged in a sack behind him, Smith kept the cast

Above: *The captured alien.*

Opposite:
The aliens' crushing attack on El Toro.

and crew immensely entertained. In general, Devlin recalls, this was the actor's much appreciated *modus operandi* and it was contagious. For example, while waiting for the camera crew to set up a unique shot that necessitated setting a Steadicam on a dolly in a moving truck, Smith and Goldblum engaged in some impromptu dancing and singing.

Another day, two of the youngest actors, Ross Bagley and Mae Whitman, entertained themselves with a Praying Mantis that had the misfortune to stow away on one of the movie trucks. Bagley and Whitman adopted it, tried to feed it potato chips and kept it in the shade of the blue tent, the only structure available to protect the cast and crew from the sun. They named the bug Jack and, after wrap, rescued their new friend from the Salt Flats, setting it free in the more temperate city of Wendover.

Despite its severe and unforgiving conditions,

the vast Salt Flats proved to be an ideal setting for one of the film's most spectacular sequences. In the script, Hiller, lugging his alien prisoner across the brilliant white desert, encounters an army of fleeing civilians, speeding across the landscape in assorted cars, mobile homes, trailers and motorcycles. At the head of this rag-tag bunch is Russell Casse, played by Randy Quaid, a wild-eyed, erratic, well-intended one-time pilot who moonlights as a crop-duster. Casse and his horde encounter Hiller. The meeting is pivotal, one of those fateful instances when two completely antithetical characters join forces.

The film-makers recruited the citizens of Wendover for this scene, who drove to the set in their own vehicles, 150 in all. Positioned against the horizon, on the word 'action' they rumbled across the salt. However, the sun, salt and sky proved a blinding mixture; the drivers couldn't see the camera positions

and veered off course. To solve this problem, a pha-lanx of production assistants lined up in the distance in front of the fleet. They then waved a combination of their arms and huge flags, thus serving as human signposts for the oncoming throng.

The company moved to Wendover Airport after completing the scenes on the Salt Flats. This location was auspicious: built in 1940 as an army air base, it housed the hangar that secreted the *Enola Gay*, the famed World War Two B-29 that dropped the atomic bomb 'Little Boy' on Hiroshima. Wendover Airport also served as the United States Air Force training facility for the 509th Composite Group, the unit that would eventually drop the bomb.

As previously mentioned, the airstrip doubled for the infamous Area 51. Opposite 'Area 51', the Wend-over Airport's broad tarmac backed up to the Utah desert, an austere vista of scrub, sand and moun-

tains, under a ribbon of sky. Like the Salt Flats, this backdrop was conducive to later effects. Specifically, a swarm of alien Attackers that darken the sky as they strafe the runway of the El Toro airbase. The Wendover airstrip became El Toro with the help of some life-size models of fighter jets and Humvees strewn across the tarmac. This El Toro reproduction looked so authentic, however, that during filming two curious F-18s buzzed the set, investigating the new airbase that somehow had appeared virtually overnight.

The airport's tarmac was also a temporary refuge for the 150 motor homes and recreational vehicles that had traversed the Salt Flats. The good citizens of Wendover set up their grills and card games in this make-shift trailer park, whilst the film-making team marshalled a monumental shot. The scene called for alien Attackers to devastate these mobile refugees and required the extras, all 470 of them, to run towards the safety of Area 51 as a firestorm of

Right: Bill Pullman, during his first day of filming, delivers a rallying speech as President Whitmore.

Below: The citizens of Wendover provided the extras needed for the convoy of survivors.

explosions rained down from the skies. Emmerich chose distinct spots on the ground that would coordinate with spaceships above, to be added to the scene in post-production. Mechanical effects supervisor Clay Pinney rigged corresponding explosive charges. Meanwhile, Dan Bradley rehearsed with his stunt team, inventing a few new moves along the way, using an air-ramp that catapulted the stunt man attached to a wire into the air as a ratchet yanked him into space.

Emmerich scheduled the shot at the 'magic hour' just before dark. Five cameras sat in various positions on the tarmac, as well as one perched on a scaffold for the master shot. Assistant directors and production assistants with bullhorns signalled the extras, who stampeded towards the master camera, as eighteen bursts of fire leapt into the sky around them in syncopated precision. Twenty-five stunt players sprinted and dove in time with erupting jeeps and trailers.

While Wendover seemed to witness a colossal conflagration on a daily basis, it also saw one of the movie's most inspiring and vital scenes, in which the President, played by Bill Pullman, rallies the troops and the nation. It is perhaps the defining moment of the film, and it was also Pullman's first day on set. This monologue took place at night, so filming began at about 6pm and ended at dawn. Cinematographer Karl Walter Lindenlaub supervised as his crew placed the camera aloft in a crane that slowly descended towards Pullman, who stood in the back of a truck as he addressed a sea of extras. Huge key lights illuminated the dark with a garish glow as smoke billowed through the set, belched from a machine behind camera. While this impressive staging underscored the significance of the powerful speech, it was not perhaps the most intimate setting in which to deliver it. Pullman, understandably, was nervous. As it turned out, he found some serendipitous comfort and enlightenment in his surroundings.

"I had never heard of Wendover before, didn't know where it was or anything about it," he recalls. "My first day of shooting was 6 August and, sitting in my hotel, I noticed that Wendover was all over the television news. Turned out that we were shooting in the Wendover Airport, where the *Enola Gay* was built, exactly fifty years after the bomb had been dropped. In the movie, there are a lot of philosoph-

ical and moral parallels between the kind of decisions that Truman had to make and the ones my character considers. Surrounded by all that history, hearing the continuing controversies relating to it, I realised the gravity of a decision like that, how dire the circumstances have to be to contemplate it."

Below and bottom: *Two of the scenes filmed at Wendover Airport.*

In The Air

Right: *The President used to be a Gulf War pilot.*

Opposite above: *The Sky Crane helicopter model*

Below: *Volker Engel, in front of a wooden F-18 mock-up.*

The military naturally plays an important role in the battle against the alien foes and one of the story's heroes is an ace Marine pilot. In fact, Will Smith studied the art of flying a fighter jet in a simulator and flew with a Marine lieutenant two months prior to production. The film-makers also sought the military's advice and blessing, which led to an interesting discovery.

"Whenever you try to do a film that involves the military, you try to get its support, especially if it is portrayed in a favourable light, as it is in our movie. This gives you access to their bases and planes, things like that," Devlin notes. "So, we approached the military early on. They enjoyed the script, but said there were a few technical problems in terms of how they work. So we addressed those issues and, actually, that really helped us to make the movie more realistic. Once we had revised the script to our satisfaction, we took it back to them. They said, 'Great, we love it. We're all set to join you, but there is one little thing. Can you remove any reference to Area 51?' Of course we couldn't because we wanted to tap into pre-existing mythology about UFOs and we couldn't do that without referring to Area 51. Because of that, the military declined to support the film."

The military's refusal to endorse the film impacted

on *Independence Day* in several ways. Initially, the visual effects department had contemplated featuring Y-F 22 Stealth fighters in some of the aerial scenes. When it seemed the military might lend its support to the film, the choice of jet planes changed accordingly.

"In the beginning, there was no talk of any military support and all of a sudden we got a message from production that we would get a lot of (their) planes," notes visual effects supervisor Volker Engel. "We would have the chance to have air-to-air footage and we could do that with F-18 jet fighter planes, so we changed our original planes from Y-F 22 Stealth fighters to F-18s. Funnily enough, that changed later because there were some questions about the script... so we didn't get the military support anyway. But we had already established the F-18s as our fighters, which I think finally was okay because I like them much better than the Y-F 22s."

The model department was called on to produce a number of F-18 fighter jets, as well as recreating several kinds of helicopters, including the gargantuan Sky Crane chopper. The actual beast, an ungainly green monster, weighing over 6,000 pounds, made an appearance at LAX. A bank of headlights, spanning twenty-five feet, extended off the sides of the helicopter, causing it to weave and dance as it lifted off. The lights were designed to flicker at specific intervals, in a vain attempt to communicate with the aliens. The Sky Crane resembled an other-worldly craft itself; some mystified residents of Victorville, California, spotted it bobbing in the sky when the technicians sent it up on a test run and reported it as a UFO to the local sheriff.

Naturally, the reticent aliens have absolutely nothing to say to the odd, blinking helicopter and blow it out of the sky. In actuality, this fate befell a miniature version of the helicopter, an intricate reproduction with real whirring propellers.

Bottom: *The live-action Sky Crane helicopter.*

Right: The F-18's brake-chute's release was simulated in front of a bluescreen, later replaced by a live-action canyon wall.

Below: 'Video-matics' were done with aluminium foil canyon walls, using a small video camera to simulate and analyse the camera moves.

The dazzling airborne battles between the powerful F-18 fighter jets and their worthy adversaries, the alien Attackers, were accomplished via Doug Smith's motion control unit and CGI. The motion control unit worked with many of the planes and spaceship models. There, the models were attached to a special computer-guided rig that allowed the craft to 'fly' through three-dimensional space. The computer also controlled the camera that pitched, rolled, tilted and panned about the aircraft, simulating flight. Once the object's flight pattern was committed to the computer's memory, Smith could duplicate it, creating additional craft from the primary one. This technique was effective for one or two shots, but it was not practical to create an entire fleet of planes this way, so these were animated creations supplied by computer graphics.

A pivotal scene in which Captain Steven Hiller,

piloting his fighter plane, is pursued by an alien Attacker through the Grand Canyon, began with an actual aerial tour, under Doug Smith's supervision. A pilot flying a World War Two training plane equipped with a camera jetted through the narrow canyon walls and the visual effects team tried to use as much of this real-life footage as possible. The pitches and rolls and patterns of a plane travelling this precarious route were committed to the computer, which guided the path of the model F-18 and Attacker attached to Smith's motion control rig accordingly.

This supersonic game of cat and mouse comes to an abrupt end when a craggy canyon wall appears directly in front of Hiller's zooming jet. To avoid this

Above left:

*Assistant pyro-
technician, Joe
Hefferman, pre-
pares the release
book for the F-18.*

Below left:

*The fighters
take to the sky.*

literal dead end, Hiller ejects and releases his brake-chute over the Attacker, blocking its pilot's view, causing it to crash. Emmerich shot Hiller's tumble to earth in the Utah desert, by suspending Will Smith, draped in a parachute, from a crane, from which he plummeted. The crash leading up to his landing was done via models, pyrotechnics and sleight of hand.

"We used a little model parachute, maybe two feet in diameter, to simulate the action of his brake-chute opening up over the Attacker," Engel explains. "An air cannon was used to blow some air into the chute, which we released by hand and the whole thing was shot in front of a blue screen, outside, to

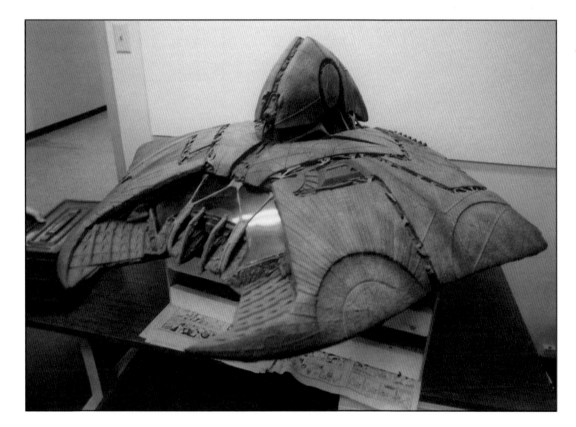

This page: *A four-foot alien Attacker.*

Opposite above left: *The fighters prepare to attack!*

Opposite above right: *A tiny ejection seat model, including pilot, is shot in front of a bluescreen.*

Opposite below: *These F-14 , F-16 and F-18 fighter models were assembled on a tarmac tabletop miniature. Pilots walking towards their planes were shot greenscreen on stage by the second unit and added in post-production.*

get the real sunlight."

In the same shot, even Will Smith was reduced to a miniature.

"We shot the pilot ejecting as a miniature in front of an outdoor blue screen," Engel adds. "The pilot was maybe four inches tall and it was rigged with a pyro device that made it look like a flame was coming out of the ejection seat, propelling Captain Hiller high into the air. This last element was added into the compositing later."

The corresponding crash landing of the Attacker began with the construction of the smashed Attacker model, dubbed 'the pizza pie', due to its large, round, flat shape.

"The pizza pie was built slightly tilted, so we could see the blue sky at the far end of the miniature," Engel says. "It was about fifteen feet wide and twenty feet deep. The surface was made of foam and the model-makers carved a trench in the middle of it, which could be filled up with sand. This made it seem more realistic, showing that when the Attacker collided with the ground, it really dug into the dirt and kicked up some huge dust clouds."

The effects team shot the crash from several different angles, utilising another Attacker, in addition to the pizza pie, which required the use of some

Above right: *The four-foot Attacker awaits its crash landing, sitting on a steel pipe as a guide track. Visual effects director of photography, Philipp Timme, discusses the sun angle with key grip, David Novak, while production assistant, Pete Novitch, cues up the video playback.*

Below right: *A four-foot Attacker is catapulted via bungee through an explosion.*

unique methods of alien transit.

"We used our four-foot Attacker and connected a wire to it, which in turn was attached to a pick-up truck," Engel recalls. "The truck dragged the Attacker through the dirt. We had added some mountains made out of foam, attached to c-stands. These were placed in the background, because we saw some in the horizon of the live action footage with Will Smith in the desert after he crash landed, as he walked towards the imaginary Attacker, which we added later in post."

Eventually, Smith actually encountered a life-sized crashed Attacker, situated in the middle of the Utah desert. Its twisted, gnarled, intricate facade seemed strangely compatible with the surreal landscape. Smith, as the enraged Captain Hiller, climbed

Above left: *One of the large-scale F-18s used for firing missiles, using model rocket motors.*

Below left: *Doug Smith supervised Anna Foerster's camera crew for the shooting of the cotton clouds used in the first dogfight.*

Right: *Flying along two guide wires and pulled by a bungee-cord, an F-18 makes a narrow escape through a fireball.*

aboard the smashed craft, encountering his first alien, face-to-face. As he reached into the cockpit, alien tentacles, operated by Patrick Tatopoulos and his puppeteers, slithered out to defend themselves.

While Captain Hiller managed to survive the dog-fight, many other fighter pilots became blazing casualties, as the Attackers blasted them from the skies. Fulfilling these airborne explosions became an elaborate, inter-departmental process.

"We used a very interesting technique to show the F-18s exploding," Engel notes. "We exploded a model F-18 on Stage 35, shooting it on film at 125 frames per second. In post-production, we took this element and positioned it exactly where we wanted

the explosion to happen in the picture and then computer graphics provided us with a jet fighter that flies through the frame and ends up directly in the exploding position. We did the same thing with a couple of motion control planes. We shot an exploding F-18 that was positioned exactly how we later wanted it to be in the movie. We gave the video of that to Doug Smith's motion control department and they made the motion control plane look like it was flying into the exact position the explosion took place."

For the planes that detonated in the Grand Canyon, the art department replicated the canyon walls, based on Smith's aerial photography. The model stood roughly twelve feet high, was made entirely of foam and provided the backdrop for an exploding plane, furnished by motion control or, sometimes, by Joe Viskocil's pyro effects department.

"We rigged a plane on wires to fly through some explosions that Joe Viskocil had rigged throughout this model Grand Canyon," Engel explains. "Whenever a plane would fly through a fireball, it was rigged on two guide wires, which were thin, metal ropes, and another wire was used to pull it through the canyon. This third wire was attached to a bungee cord and when it was released from this cord, it would burst through the flames. Joe Viskocil would eyeball the speed of the plane and trigger the explosion at the exactly correct moment, after it had been released from the bungee cord."

Above: *Pyrotechnician, Emmet Kane, prepares a small F-18 model to be blown up during the first dogfight.*

Left: *Emmet Kane (on ladder) prepares an F-18 for the deadly impact, watched by pyrotechnics effects supervisor, Joe Viskocil (left).*

The Mother Ship

Right: Production designer, Oliver Scholl, inspects the detailing on the big cone inside the Mother Ship.

During the film's tense finale, Will Smith and Jeff Goldblum have to enter the Mother Ship and dock their captured Attacker. The colossal Mother Ship, which served as the cavernous docking bay for hundreds of Attackers, was also the headquarters in which the aliens hatched their complex, computer-driven plans to take over the world. Creating the Mother Ship required several different, elaborate models, as Mike Joyce's crew not only had to construct the exterior craft, but also the spooky interior passages through which the Attackers

entered and docked.

The actual Mother Ship model was an elaborate creation that immediately sailed over to Doug Smith's motion control unit. Smith's two motion control crews shot most of the Mother Ship footage, including the exterior Mother Ship and interior point-of-view shots, as Attackers flew through the vast internal tunnels. Smith's department also filmed these Attackers anytime they were in frame, but Anna Foerster, under Volker Engel's supervision, handled all the shots involving a docking Attacker, while Philipp Timme lensed all the scenes with aliens inside the Mother Ship.

Once settled in Smith's domain, the twelve-foot Mother Ship model was secured to the motion control rig and shot with the slow-moving motion control camera, to simulate the movement of an Attacker entering the Mother Ship. The Mother Ship's tunnel that Joyce's model unit provided was approximately twenty feet long and five feet wide and the clever model-makers designed it so that

Left: The twelve-foot Mother Ship model during construction.

Opposite below: Model-maker, Ken Swenson, checking the lights on the Mother Ship's alien control booth.

Below: The holes in the Mother Ship model will be filled with tiny Destroyers.

portions could be moved through the structure. For instance, ten pieces of tunnel ceiling were variously dislodged while the camera crane slowly drove through the miniature Mother Ship.

The motion control process is deliberate and painstaking and some of the passes took seven hours to accomplish.

"The camera was only able to shoot one frame every couple of seconds, because of the great depth of field," Smith notes. "We wanted the tunnel in focus in front of camera and also in focus twenty feet away from camera, so that took a long time."

The interior Mother Ship was punctuated by a labyrinth of pillars, but the visual effects team discovered that they did not necessarily need to construct three-dimensional columns to illustrate the effect.

"We actually only built one full column, two half-columns and then a couple of background ones were produced as a photo-backing. That is, one column was photographed and it was enlarged to the size of a column, it was cut out and pasted on to some ply-

wood and we could use those in the background," Engel explains. "The whole Mother Ship interior was shot in very heavy smoke, which also enabled us to use the photo-backing columns in the background, because it sufficiently obscured them."

Final Attack

Jeff Goldblum's plan to disable the Destroyers' shields provides the Earth's forces with a glimmer of hope for defeating the aliens and leads to the movie's second major dogfight. This, Engel comments, "was not that much different from the first dogfight, technically. We had to shoot a lot of background plates to put in CG or motion control jet fighters or motion control Attackers. The main difference was that most of the dogfight took place beneath the underbelly of the Destroyer, meaning between the underbelly and the desert landscape, around Area 51."

The logistics of this battle meant that the model shop had to create a miniature desert to juxtapose beneath the Destroyer. This vast landscape appeared as a circular table, about fifteen feet in diameter, complete with desert and mountain topography, carved out of hard foam. The desert sat against an airbrushed vista of sky, clouds and distant peaks, above which hovered the twelve-foot Destroyer, itself mounted on a pylon that allowed it to rotate. The distance between desert and Destroyer was only about twelve inches, which necessitated the use of a low profile camera, so named because it is a slim seven inches.

Like the first dogfight, this second aerial conflict relied on several live action scenes, specifically the principal actors in the cockpit of a fighter jet, engaged in battle with the aliens. This was achieved by the use of a gimbal, which rocked the mock-plane, piloted by the actor, in front of a moving sky backdrop. Cued flashes of light and sparks flew by, representing alien blasts. This classic film technique has lately been usurped by the blue or green screen, an 'improvement' that is not always cost effective, as Engel points out:

"For this movie, Roland felt it would be a good idea to use painted backdrops, large pieces of canvas mounted behind the cockpits, and to have interactive lighting on the actors when they were in the cockpit, when alien light balls fly past them. They even took some hits, provided by the pyro-crew. If it hadn't been done that way, it would've meant that we had another fifty-plus shots for digital compositing to put sky backdrops as aerial photography behind the actors."

UFO's

Although modern sightings date back only to 1947, there is evidence to support the theory that UFOs have been seen throughout history. However, it was in 1947 that the term flying saucer was first coined, by Kenneth Arnold, a civilian pilot. As he was flying over the Cascade Mountains in Washington State, Arnold's attention was caught by some bright lights. He then noticed a 'V' formation of 'aircraft', which seemed to have no wings. Arnold later reported the incident at Yakima and described the UFO he'd seen as moving "like a saucer would if you skipped it across water." And so the world was introduced to flying saucers.

Most Unidentified Flying Objects are eventually explained away. But what about that small portion for which there isn't an easy explanation? There have been literally millions of sightings, also known as Close Encounters of the First Kind, since 1947. Surely there have been too many for there not to be something out there? UFOlogists certainly believe so, but, as yet, there is no hard proof. Sightings of UFOs by astronauts also became so common that NASA invented a term for them — bogeys.

They have certainly proved popular in the cinema with titles like *The Flying Saucer*, *Earth vs. The Flying Saucers*, the documentary *Unidentified Flying Objects* and *The UFO Incident*. ■

Previous page top: *The cockpit mock-up is rolled into the hangar for filming with the actors in front of a large painted canvas.*

Previous page centre: *The twelve-foot Destroyer closes in on Area 51.*

Previous page bottom: *CG effects add scores of alien Attackers to the sky around the Destroyer.*

As mentioned, the CG unit played an integral part in the various aerial battles. The seemingly endless supply of alien spaceships careening out of the sky could only be accomplished by computer graphic imagery, a painstaking process that ultimately pulled a devastating fleet of flyers out of the thin air of cyberspace.

"There were several shots, for example, where CG fighter planes were to be added to the foregrounds or backgrounds of a previously photographed plate,"

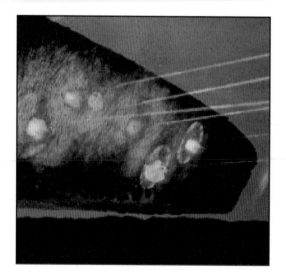

digital effects producer Tricia Ashford notes. "We accomplished this by first creating skeletons to match the basic shape of each aircraft. These models were created by picking points on scale models of the aircraft and converting each point into a coordinate in 3D space. The set of these points, when complete, defines the outer surface or skin of the object. We also used reference photography of actual aircraft to texture-map the 3D models in the computer. By stretching and fitting digitised photographs of each section of the aircraft, the object could be viewed from any angle and appear just as the original aircraft. Virtual lights were then placed in space and coloured, just like practical lights, to simulate the environment of the practical plate."

After the computer-generated fighter jet was born and properly lit, Ashford's crew had to make it fly, via carefully choreographed camera moves. Or, as Ashford puts it:

"Our next step was to match the virtual camera to the practical camera that it had to mimic. (Computer graphics supervisor) Tara Turner wrote a translation algorithm that took the input of the recorded data for lens, focal length, position and

angle of the practical camera. Then, we positioned the synthetic camera to the corresponding position. If the practical camera moved, then we simply described the motion in the computer and, with a little refinement, we matched it exactly."

In theory, this provided the blueprint for the aerial battles. However, Emmerich did not envision small skirmishes. This was a battle of galactic proportions. In practice, this notion "demanded that we employ newer, revolutionary techniques that were written especially for this production," Ashford observes.

VisionArt's Josh Rose and Rob Bredlow, at Ashford's behest, provided one of those techniques, "intelligent, flocking algorithms" that basically described the flight capabilities of each aircraft, human and alien, in a terrifically idiosyncratic way. Essentially, this program allowed Emmerich to 'direct' the battles in cyberspace.

"They wrote descriptions that gave each craft an individual 'personality' that defined such fighting characteristics as how often and to which direction they would turn when pursued, how they would choose and lock onto their targets and at what

range they would fire their weapons," Ashford explains. "By doing this, we were able to run hundreds of virtual dogfights in the computer, choose the best moments and then strategically position the virtual camera to capture them. We would also, as required, add hand animated hero aircraft to the foreground when we needed them to perform a specific manoeuvre in the storyline. This type of production method gave Roland and Dean the flexibility they needed when editing the movie."

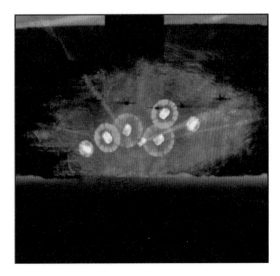

Above: Effects were used to enhance the scenes involving real pyrotechnics – here, a plane narrowly escapes the exploding airfield.

Opposite above: CG effects give the impression of a vast fleet of planes.

Left and opposite below: Effects fill the sky with explosions during the alien attack.

End Game

The denouement of the movie comes as, on 4 July, the military might of the Earth combines with Levinson's computer genius to destroy the alien threat. In a final daring feat of bravery, Steve and David take the captured alien Attacker from Area 51 into the docking station of the Mother Ship to plant a computer virus in their communication system and fire a nuclear missile. At the same time, President Whitmore leads the largest aerial battle in man's history against the Destroyers.

For the final Destroyer crash, the visual effects department rigged up large plywood pieces at a forty-five degree angle. A fiery explosion was then triggered at the base to crawl up the plywood. In post-production, many different elements were pasted together to become the underbelly of the burning Destroyer.

This brings to a conclusion *Independence Day*'s spectacular visual effects work. They are amongst some of the most impressive seen on screen. As Captain Steven Hiller says to Dylan, "Didn't I promise you fireworks?"

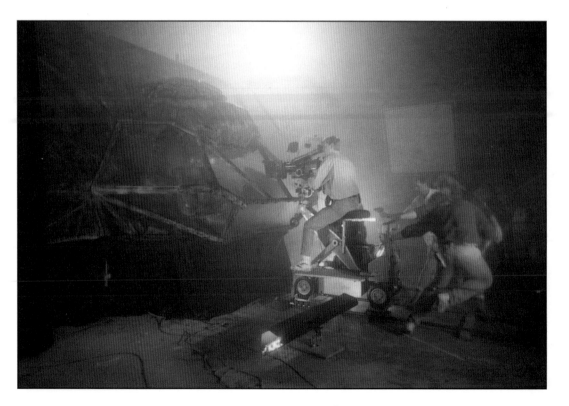

Above left:
Working on the fiery explosion of the Destroyer crash at the end of the movie.

Below left:
President Whitmore leads the final battle against the aliens.

ID4
INDEPENDENCE DAY

The Cast

Cpt. Steven Hiller	Will Smith
President Whitmore	Bill Pullman
David Levinson	Jeff Goldblum
Marilyn Whitmore	Mary McDonnell
Julius Levinson	Judd Hirsch
Constance Spano	Margaret Colin
Russell Casse	Randy Quaid
General Grey	Robert Loggia
Secretary Nimziki	James Rebhorn
Marty Gilbert	Harvey Fierstein
Jasmine Dubrow	Vivica A. Fox
Miguel Casse	James Duval
Troy Casse	Guiseppe Andrews
Alicia Casse	Lisa Jakub
Dylan	Ross Bagley
Patricia Whitmore	Mae Whitman
Doctor Brakish Okun	Brent Spiner
Cpt. Jimmy Wilder	Harry Connick Jr

The Film-makers

Director	Roland Emmerich
Produced by	Dean Devlin
Written by	Dean Devlin & Roland Emmerich
Executive Producers	Roland Emmerich, Ute Emmerich & William Fay
Director of Photography	Karl Walter Lindenlaub, BVK
Production Designers	Patrick Tatopoulos & Oliver Scholl
Film Editor	David Brenner
Music by	David Arnold
Visual Effects	Volker Engel & Douglas Smith
Costume Designer	Joseph Porro

(The above credits are not all-inclusive and do not necessarily reflect final billing.)